Snowflake Security

Securing Your Snowflake
Data Cloud

Ben Herzberg
Yoav Cohen

Apress®

Snowflake Security: Securing Your Snowflake Data Cloud

Ben Herzberg
Modiin, Israel

Yoav Cohen
Ness-Ziona, Israel

ISBN-13 (pbk): 978-1-4842-7388-3
https://doi.org/10.1007/978-1-4842-7389-0

ISBN-13 (electronic): 978-1-4842-7389-0

Managing Director, Apress Media LLC: Welmoed Spahr
Acquisitions Editor: Susan McDermott
Development Editor: Laura Berendson
Coordinating Editor: Jessica Vakili

Cover designed by eStudioCalamar

Cover image designed by Pixabay

Distributed to the book trade worldwide by Springer Science+Business Media New York, 1 New York Plaza, New York, NY 10004. Phone 1-800-SPRINGER, fax (201) 348-4505, e-mail orders-ny@springer-sbm.com, or visit www.springeronline.com. Apress Media, LLC is a California LLC and the sole member (owner) is Springer Science + Business Media Finance Inc (SSBM Finance Inc). SSBM Finance Inc is a **Delaware** corporation.

For information on translations, please e-mail booktranslations@springernature.com; for reprint, paperback, or audio rights, please e-mail bookpermissions@springernature.com.

Apress titles may be purchased in bulk for academic, corporate, or promotional use. eBook versions and licenses are also available for most titles. For more information, reference our Print and eBook Bulk Sales web page at http://www.apress.com/bulk-sales.

Any source code or other supplementary material referenced by the author in this book is available to readers on GitHub via the book's product page, located at www.apress.com/978-1-4842-7388-3. For more detailed information, please visit http://www.apress.com/source-code.

Printed on acid-free paper

This book is dedicated to my beloved family. Thanks for supporting me throughout this – Tal, Yoray, Shira, and Ori. I'd also like to thank my parents and siblings for always sticking up for me.

—Ben "Green Dragon" Herzberg

This book is dedicated to Maya, Emma, Ethan, Eviatar, and Eliana, my co-founders in life.

—Yoav Cohen

Table of Contents

About the Authors

Ben Herzberg is an experienced hacker and developer with years of experience in endpoint security, behavioral analytics, application security, and data security. His professional experience in development, research, and security includes roles such as the CTO of Cynet and leading the threat research group at Imperva. Ben is now the Chief Scientist for Satori, streamlining data access and security with DataSecOps.

Ben also loves to write, speak at conferences, travel, and meet new people.

Yoav Cohen is the Co-founder and Chief Technology Officer of Satori Cyber. At Satori, Yoav is building the company's technology vision and leading the research and engineering teams. Before founding Satori Cyber, Yoav was the Senior Vice President of Product Development for Imperva, which he joined as part of the acquisition of Incapsula, a cloud-based web applications security and acceleration company, where he was the Vice President of Engineering. Before joining Incapsula, Yoav held several technology leadership positions at SAP.

When he isn't glued to his laptop or on a whiteboard, Yoav can be found traveling with his wife and four kids in an RV, playing electric guitar, or doing laps at the pool. He is still dreaming about building his own operating system.

Yoav holds an M.Sc. in Computer Science and a B.Sc. in Computer Science and Biology from Tel-Aviv University.

About the Technical Reviewers

Chris Edge has been working in IT for his whole career, starting off in various back-office roles, such as document management (ISO/BS standards), networks, and infrastructure, before learning that dealing with all things data related was the perfect job for him!

Chris has been working in the analytics domain now for over 25 years, having been instrumental in setting up many greenfield sites incorporating various database, ETL, and reporting technologies over the last two and a half decades, and helping to steer companies that are mid-flight and looking for new ways of working.

Chris is one of the three partners of Leading Edge IT, a consultancy dealing with all things data, focusing on strategy and execution, focused in the cloud.

Chris Tabb started his career in the business intelligence/analytics domain 25 years ago, beginning at Cognos in the 1990s working in the back-office before becoming an expert in all their products and leaving to become an independent BI consultant in 1998. It is safe to say he loves data and always has.

He has followed the evolution of the analytics industry, working hands-on with all the technologies in the ecosystem: databases, ETL/ELT, BI/OLAP/visualization tools, big data technologies, and infrastructure on-premises/cloud across many vendors, some old, some new.

Nowadays, he works at a more strategic level providing technical roadmap, vendor selection, migration strategies, data management, and data and application architecture, but he still likes to keep hands-on with products in the data ecosystem. He also actively participates in podcasts and posts where he provides his views and insights into the data world using #DataTips.

Ian Chotakoo has worked in the IT industry across multiple sectors including defense, retail, banking, and manufacturing.

He has been part of the full development life cycle with a focus on data, leadership, complex delivery, and commercial awareness to influence and ensure successful business outcomes.

Ian holds a B.Sc. in Information Technology and Business Information Systems, having fallen in love with technology while growing up in the 1980s.

Acknowledgments

Writing a book about a product that develops fast, the way Snowflake does, is challenging. It is shooting at a moving target, and throughout this project, we were glad to have a lot of help from different sources.

Our energies on writing this book started at home with our families, who gave us their full support to work on this project despite working full capacity on Satori. Writing this took away some of our weekends and nights, and we're hoping to give them some of this time back as soon as we find a way to time travel.

We went on a mission to help companies achieve better DataSecOps and to help them solve security and governance challenges in an agile way using Satori. During our work with many data-driven companies, we spent a lot of time trying to understand and help others understand how to secure their data stores better, and Snowflake in particular. That was also when we understood there was a need for this book.

This project couldn't have happened without the immense support we got from Satori. This help was both directly by giving us the time and assistance in working on this project and indirectly by giving us the emotional support we needed for taking on such a challenge while also staying focused on our company mission. In Satori, many people helped us throughout this journey. We would like to specifically thank Eldad Chai, Satori's Co-founder and CEO, and David Levin, Satori's Head of Product, for their help.

We've had great help from Chris Edge, Chris Tabb, and Ian Chotakoo from Leading Edge IT, a leading (as the name implies :)) Snowflake solution partner. They took part in the technical editing of this book. They also went well above that in greatly supporting this project since its incubation and until it was ready to publish. Their vast experience and knowledge around Snowflake made their help unparalleled.

From Snowflake itself, we've had some great insights and support from several people, including Vikas Jain, Omer Singer, Kent Graziano, Seth Youssef, Jonathan Sander, David "BigDataDave" Spezia, Felipe Hoffa, and several others. Their help included discussions about new features and several capabilities, which allowed us to focus our efforts on this project. In addition, they were patient and fun to work with, making this interaction all the more enjoyable.

Foreword

Once upon a time, businesses waited to worry about the security of their data stack until their employees, customers, or board told them about a problem. In today's world, the responsible business or technology leader needs to be proactive. Decisions about securing data are foundational and impact everything from how employees or vendors are onboarded to the way reports are distributed, new systems are deployed, and workflows are designed. Why? Because today all businesses run on data.

I have been working to launch software businesses in the tech and media industries since the 1990s. It is rare to find enterprise software that makes teams want to use it more as the business grows, gets more complex, and operations scale. Here is the secret sauce. Sales and support teams are the first to see and hear what customers need to be "successful." The game changer is when those needs are communicated to the tech team. Any cloud data platform provider can help their customer learn to use their product in the way the provider intended. Few can build for what their unique customer needs and then deliver that capability at scale. Ultimately, it's the engineering leadership that must deliver on the promise to meet customers' needs. That willingness to partner on building and delivering is rare.

I first heard about Snowflake in 2016. Several of my peers who were leading large data teams at other companies had started to comment on the performance they were getting with their queries. I had just moved to Seattle to build out a new data team. At the time, I was consumed with hiring, finding data sources, doing the basic reporting, creating a data model, and keeping pace with newly launched online retail businesses hungry for data. I like to be the early adopter. But it felt like too much of a lift to bring in a new data platform.

Then it was 2018, and this was a perfect opportunity. I was grappling with how to integrate a fragmented legacy data infrastructure and a tech org with the dual performance dilemma of frequent systems performance problems and fewer resources than required to supply stakeholders with data. By the end of that first proof of concept, we saw the promise that Snowflake could address all three issues. So, the crucial next step was ensuring whether we could meet our high hurdle for data security. Performance at scale is the entry point for B2B technology providers with any global enterprise, but trust and security are the true differentiators. I believe that Snowflake has both.

Now in 2021, I read or hear about companies and organizations using or misusing data in some new way. Staying fluent in how information moves through an organization and its IT systems is typically not easy. In most organizations, people mainly care only about the information and tools they rely on to get their work done. Nearly every organization has some amount of "shadow IT" in marketing, finance, customer service, operations, etc., based on individual preferences and the aspiration "to move quickly and break things" or "be a disruptor." But what happens when the systems in the shadows that once met a burning need are orphaned? I think it's an interesting question to ask, and while I don't necessarily have a point of view on the solution, I know at least a part of the resulting scenario is a risk.

Fragmentation in the fabric of enterprise technology creates risk with an increased likelihood of error, corruption, misuse, or theft. When you start to look at how much data organizations have started accumulating directly or through third parties, the implications of poor data security become staggering.

Yoav and Ben are helping a lot of organizations with these challenges every day across all sorts of technologies, and now they seek to educate people on Snowflake. They've been working on these issues as operators for a long time. Satori was created to build the tools and integration capabilities they wish they'd had so that tech leaders can be better informed about the data security risks in their organizations and make better-informed decisions on how to resolve them.

This guide is written from the perspective of people who understand you're trying to manage risk in an entire organization, not just one tool or platform. They understand the decisions, policies, and other factors that go into making the modern enterprise security strategy successful. They also understand not everyone who may need to become an expert starts out that way.

Overall, the more businesses and tech leaders care about and want to understand data security to protect their employees and customers, the better off we will be for it going forward.

—**Anita Lynch**
VP, Data Governance, Disney Streaming

Introduction

We have been fighting cyber attacks and helping organizations defend themselves from cyber attacks for most of our careers. With cybercriminals, hacktivists, state-sponsored attackers, and insider threats, organizations are at risk of having their data stolen, leaked, or misused. But it doesn't take a sophisticated hacker to put your organization at risk – breach of compliance or not meeting contractual obligations can create damage as well.

An effective program to maintain your data properly secured and governed relies on multiple layers of defense and includes, among others, application security, network security, and endpoint security. However, at the core of your organization's strategy to secure and govern data lies the data store – a database, cloud file system, data warehouse, data lake, or any of the other forms of technology used to store your organization's data.

In recent years, and as part of our work building Satori, a startup company with the mission of simplifying data governance, we've seen Snowflake grow in popularity, being adopted by organizations small and large. Snowflake is fantastic – it just works, and it does what it does exceptionally well. In addition, it brings with it many features to secure and govern your data. Still, like many other *Something as a Service* like SaaS, IaaS, PaaS, and DBaaS, there's a shared responsibility between you, the customer, and the vendor, in our case, Snowflake, to ensure your data is safe.

You'd be surprised (or not?), but most data leaks are not the result of a Mission Impossible Ethan Hunt rappelling down into a data center stealing encrypted hard drives and decrypting them on NSA supercomputers. Although we are certain such events do occur, most attacks usually target the weakest link in your defenses: employees who are reusing passwords for multiple platforms, permissions to database objects that were never revoked, credentials you provisioned for some script someone urgently needed a while back and were left unattended, and so on. This is not meant to cause you despair and make you feel like a lot can go wrong (though a lot *can* go wrong); it's intended as good news – there are plenty of simple steps you can take to reduce your risk.

We know it can be overwhelming and that sometimes it feels like keeping data secure is an impossible task. However, from our experience, the best way to systematically identify and fortify your weakest links is to be able to reason about the security and governance of your data more logically, focusing your attention on a single domain at a time. But where to get started? Is there a playbook to follow?

The goal of this book is to provide you with a framework to reason about the security and governance of your data on Snowflake, to understand what Snowflake is doing and what's left for you to do, and give you a playbook, which, if followed, can take your data on Snowflake to the next level of security and governance.

While this book focuses on Snowflake, the principles laid out throughout this book can be applied to other data store technologies. Each has its own features and capabilities regarding security and governance, and there are a host of tools you can use to complement or simplify the process.

Who Is This Book For?

We wrote this book for the people responsible for implementing data security and governance controls on Snowflake, whether they are experienced Snowflake administrators looking for a checklist or evaluating Snowflake as their next data store technology and understanding how they can migrate data safely to that new environment. The book is a valuable resource for data engineers, database administrators, DataOps/DataSecOps engineers, security practitioners, and anyone interested in learning more about securing data in the cloud with Snowflake.

Prerequisites

This book will not teach you "everything you need to know" about Snowflake itself. However, it *is* a book about Snowflake security, and we do expect readers to have at least basic knowledge of Snowflake, SQL, and so on. You can find resources for learning Snowflake online, and we've listed a few good ones on this book's website (`https://snowflake-security.com`).

Staying Focused

Snowflake offers a lot of different ways to do things. For example, you can use its web UI to change your configuration or use SQL commands. In addition, you have a lot of optional parameters you *may* configure. And there is a vast amount of metadata you can use when analyzing your account activity.

As we believe in the old saying that "if you chase two rabbits, you will lose them both," and because this is a book and not documentation, we would like to stay focused and made the following decisions:

- Though occasionally we will show how to do things using the web UI, our preference will be to use SQL commands. The main reason is that using the SQL commands is more effective at scale and that using the web UI is more self-explanatory.

- Snowflake integrates with multiple cloud platforms and third-party services. It would exceed the scope of this book in providing a detailed explanation or example of each. We chose the most popular ones and tried to convey the principles and logic behind each topic rather than replace the official documentation.

Reference Material

We've included the code samples in this book in a git repository to clone and expand and contribute to helping others. Our git repository is at `https://github.com/SnowflakeSecurityBook`.

With this book, we're also publishing a page with some resources at `https://snowflake-security.com`. Though we can only commit to a best-effort level of updates, we will add more resources to the book's website to keep it quite up to date.

Snowflake has excellent documentation at `https://docs.snowflake.com`, which you should use in conjunction with this book. In addition, we advise you to visit the docs site from time to time to read up on new features and changes.

The Snowflake community site at `https://community.snowflake.com` is where you can ask questions and interact with other Snowflake users. Sign up to the community site to get email updates on upcoming behavior changes you need to be aware of. Another excellent opportunity to engage with the Snowflake community is to join a Snowflake user group at `https://usergroups.snowflake.com`.

Yoav often refers to himself jokingly as a software archeologist for his love of learning not just about the technology but also how it came to be. If you share that passion and want to learn more about how Snowflake was founded and the philosophy behind their innovation, we recommend you check out *Rise of the Data Cloud* by **Frank Slootman** and **Steve Hamm**.

What's Happening to Data?

Before diving into the different security controls and considerations specific to Snowflake, we felt it would be helpful to give a short overview of the ongoing transformation happening in the data processing industry. This is by no means a comprehensive description of these changes, which would deserve a book on its own, but nonetheless gives a frame of reference for Snowflake and the considerations about its security.

Over the last decade, more data is collected and from more sources. The reasons for this vary, but we'll mention some of the key ones:

- The rapid growth in the amount of data sent from billions of IoT devices and millions of applications.

- Data science libraries and tools are common and straightforward to use, enabling organizations to make value from data in an easier way that encourages more people to use the data.

- A great variety of technologies make it easier to collect, process, and store data, especially in the cloud.

The essence can be understood from the following simplified figure. Having more data to collect forces the industry to make better technology to handle this data, enabling more teams to use the data, which then feeds the beast by collecting more data.

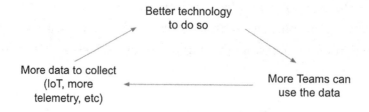

The data collected is used to analyze the past and predict the future and no longer by a relatively small number of data consumers within an organization. Many different teams attempt to take advantage of as much data processing as possible.

For example, a travel booking company may use data about its users, some of it collected by the company itself, by looking at order history, search history, reviews history, and so on. Some of it is enriched from third-party sources. The data is then used to predict what types of offers will convert best for each customer. By leveraging as much data as possible, the company can increase revenue and provide better service.

This means that more data consumers will want to use the data and not just increase sales. HR wants to predict employee attrition, customer success wants to know which customers might churn, etc. This means that being data driven is not solely the realm of the big tech giants who are always at the forefront of technology. Still, mainstream industries can and are benefitting from data analytics.

This creates security challenges in managing the massive amount of data processed by these companies on platforms such as Snowflake. What makes it even more difficult is that data is a moving target. It keeps changing as more data of different data types are sent to the cloud, transformed, or cloned and as more data consumers are using it.

The security challenges intensify as smaller teams are expected to meet the demands of data owners and data consumers and security, governance, and privacy teams.

Where Snowflake Fits In

Even before the age of big data and predictive analytics, organizations used data to make sense of and analyze their operations – sales pipeline, manufacturing productivity, and marketing campaigns, for example. But with data locked in different database systems that do not talk to each other, organizations needed a place to model and store their data to make it readily available for analysis. That place is the data warehouse. It is a database system optimized for loading large amounts of data using a standard structure to query it in many different ways easily.

Snowflake, the data cloud, was designed from the ground up to take advantage of the elasticity and scalability of the public cloud. Founded in 2012 by Mike Speiser of Sutter Hill Ventures, with co-founders Benoit Dageville, Marcin Zukowski, and Thierry Cruanes, Snowflake set out to eliminate the cost of owning your own data infrastructure, which at the time was a multimillion dollar investment in hardware, software licenses, and personnel.

Before Snowflake, the only way to increase the storage capacity of your data solution was to add servers with the additional storage capacity and relatively expensive computing power or central processing units (CPUs). Snowflake identified that computing power and storage capacity did not have to expand at the same rate. Instead, they took advantage of the public cloud's ability to provision storage independently of computing to break that paradigm and make scaling out a data solution much more cost-effective.

Another challenge that data warehouse owners faced was handling peak workloads – those times where you need to crunch a lot more data in much less time. Organizations either had to own data warehouses that sat idle 90% of the time to sustain those peak workloads or jump through hoops like manually stopping all other data processing activities when a big job was submitted. With the cloud's ability to connect more compute power to existing storage, Snowflake enables organizations to spin up as much computing power as needed to handle peak workloads and tear them back down later in a pay-for-use model. No more upfront costs for resources that are not being fully utilized.

With its lower cost of ownership, improved performance, and flexible scalability, Snowflake perfectly fits today's needs, where organizations collect more data than ever, and data analytics is at the core of every digitally transformed business.

Why Snowflake Security?

Given the considerable growth in companies taking advantage of Snowflake to store and process their data, and as a lot of this data is sensitive for different reasons (business secrets, PII, PHI, and more), we felt it would be helpful to write a book dedicated to keeping this data secure. We felt this would be especially useful since, in many cases, the Snowflake administrators in organizations are data engineers and not security experts.

The Importance of Data Security

Data is, in many cases, the biggest asset that a company has or at least one of the top resources. However, in addition to providing an immense value, data is also a significant liability in many cases. For example, holding PII of data subjects can give the company a competitive edge, incur risk (for instance, in case of a data breach), and require meeting specific regulatory and other compliance requirements.

That is why the security architecture of a data solution is, in most cases, as important as the software architecture and should be part of the design of data handling in the organization and should not be an afterthought.

Shared Responsibility Model

One of the key selling points of Snowflake is that it's a SaaS product, where you don't deal with many of the underlying infrastructures. This has benefits in reducing the amount of data engineering work you have to do. It also reduces the security surface you are responsible for, as Snowflake is accountable for some security risks.

This means that in some of the cases, security will be handled out of the box by Snowflake or the public cloud providers (at the time of writing: AWS, GCP, and Azure), some will be provided by Snowflake but need to be configured by you, and for some, you will need to add on top of what's provided by Snowflake. This is outlined throughout the book, but the essence is

- Infrastructure security is provided by the different public cloud providers where your Snowflake data is stored.

- Snowflake handles data encryption at rest.

- Snowflake provides several tools and features around authentication and authorization which you will need to configure and, in some cases, build on top of what Snowflake offers.

- Data access is encrypted out of the box, and you may also want to add network policies or other security controls on top of your data access.

Meet ACME Candy Industries

By now, you probably have a tingling feeling that you'd like to start experimenting and not just discuss theories. Even if you already have a Snowflake account, we suggest using a separate account just for experimenting with the examples and concepts throughout the book.

Throughout this book, the examples we will give are those of ACME Candy Industries, a fictitious company dealing with producing the ultimate candies. And snacks. This demo organization will provide continuity throughout the book, but the issues ACME Candy Industries is facing should apply to other areas outside of candy making.

Let's Get Started

Snowflake has many exciting security features, and it's tempting to focus on the shiny objects first. But most of the value can be derived from a few basic things, which if you get right will reduce your overall risk in a big way. As a junior software engineer, Yoav once asked a software architect what software architecture is. He said it was "the things that are harder to change later on." Although it's possible to change almost everything in your data warehouse design, there are some things that if you get right at the onset make everything else much easier down the road. So what is the road going to look like?

In Chapters 1 and 2, we will discuss structuring of your Snowflake organization, as well as the Snowflake infrastructure security, and some of the decisions you will need to make around the foundations of your Snowflake activity.

Chapter 3 will discuss Snowflake's encryption and ingestion security aspects. Much of it is educational, to know what happens "behind the scenes" to protect your data, but in other parts, it will help you with making decisions.

Once you nail down the fundamentals, it's time to think about how to organize your data. Much like a physical warehouse, there needs to be logic behind where everything is, to make it easy to find what you're looking for, and, in the context of security and data governance, set the right gateways and checkpoints before data can be used. In Chapter 4, we will discuss authentication. In Chapter 5, we will discuss network access control. In Chapter 6, we will discuss authorization.

A large part of a healthy security posture is the ability to understand what's going on and act fast when things are not going as planned. Chapter 7 will discuss auditing and monitoring and will go through the sources from which you can get metadata about your Snowflake usage, as well as how to monitor the data. Throughout the chapter, we're including examples of queries that can retrieve helpful information to improve your security level.

Finally, in Chapters 8 and 9, we will discuss two specific topics – the specific options in which you can securely share data between different Snowflake accounts, within and outside of your organization, and the ability to use Snowflake for a security data lake solution.

CHAPTER 1

Snowflake Organization Structure

Snowflake offers organizations with a rich topology of objects to help manage larger and more complex data infrastructures, while simplifying topics like billing, invoicing, database replication, and more. At the root of each Snowflake deployment lies the organization object. Organizations are a logical entity, not tied to any specific cloud provider or region.

Prior to introducing the organization's feature, the topmost object of a Snowflake deployment was the account, which was associated with a specific cloud provider or region. For example, `https://acme.snowflakecomputing.com` is a Snowflake account owned by ACME Candies, hosted in Amazon Web Service (AWS) in the North Virginia region (us-east-1). Accounts contain databases, which contain schemas, which contain tables, views, and other database objects. Should you be using a single or multiple accounts?

1.1. Single Account vs. Multiple Accounts

There's no doubt that managing multiple accounts means more work for you: because organizations are a relatively new concept in Snowflake, much of the work you do on one account would need to be done on your other accounts as well. That includes defining users and roles, integrating with an external authentication service, monitoring, and so on. However, we believe that the benefits of a multi-account strategy outweigh the short-term simplicity of a single account strategy, mostly because of the strong separation

© Ben Herzberg, Yoav Cohen 2022
B. Herzberg and Y. Cohen, *Snowflake Security*, https://doi.org/10.1007/978-1-4842-7389-0_1

it provides which you can leverage to your advantage. There are multiple factors to consider when designing a multi-account strategy:

- **Separation between different environments** – Many data engineering teams are adopting practices from software engineering such as introducing changes in a development or testing environment before they are moved to production, in an attempt to test these changes in less critical environments first. In addition, locating different environments on different accounts can enable you to choose a different balance between productivity and security risk for each environment independently.

- **Separation between different businesses** – Many large organizations are global now, with subsidiaries all around the world. Providing each subsidiary with its own Snowflake account can help overcome challenges of a fragmented IT environment. For example, a subsidiary that has regulatory constraints from using a specific cloud provider or region, or a business that has not yet migrated its identity and access system to a centralized one, controlled by global IT.

- **Data sovereignty** – Unless your business is very local, operating in just a single geographic area or jurisdiction, at some point you'll need to consider restricting certain data to specific geographic locations, which means you'll need a separate account in each of these regions.

- **Multi-cloud** – Many organizations today have a strategy for operating on more than one cloud provider, either to reduce dependency on a single vendor or as a result of acquiring or merging with other organizations that happen to operate on a different cloud provider.

- **Cost** – Because each account is associated with its own pricing plan, you can decide which feature set is required for you in each account. For example, in a production environment, you might want a higher-grade feature set, while a dev environment might have different requirements.

1.1.1. Scaling Multiple Accounts Management

Until recently, one of the hassles about managing multiple accounts was that the process of provisioning the accounts themselves (adding new accounts for your organization, as well as modifying or deleting them) was hard to automate. This made things cumbersome, especially when your organization had multiple different business units which you wanted to separate to different accounts. This left you with a choice between having more accounts but more data engineering overhead and less accounts which sometimes causes a less simplified approach when administering the accounts.

Nowadays, Snowflake allows you to manage your organization's account by using the ORGADMIN role. The ORGADMIN role enables you to create accounts or modify them easily. For example, if ACME Candies wants to set up a new staging account, they can run the following command using an ORGADMIN role:

```
CREATE ACCOUNT stage2
ADMIN_NAME = stageadmin
ADMIN_PASSWORD = '<PASSWORD>'
FIRST_NAME = stage
LAST_NAME = admin
MUST_CHANGE_PASSWORD = TRUE
EMAIL = 'dataops@acmecandies.com'
EDITION = standard
REGION = aws_us_east_1
REGION_GROUP = PUBLIC;
```

1.2. Choosing the Right Pricing Plan

At the time of writing this book, Snowflake offers four pricing plans each with its own feature set and price point. The higher-grade plans offer security-oriented features such as private link connectivity, bring-your-own-keys encryption, and even dedicated virtual servers. We won't discuss the specifics of these features in the context of choosing the right pricing plan, because pricing plans tend to change often and you can switch pricing plans at any time. However, based on what we'll discuss in the remainder of this chapter, you'll have a pretty good idea of which pricing plan is right for each one of your accounts. When in doubt, we suggest to start low and move up as needed. The great thing about Snowflake's business model is that you pay as you go and don't need to commit upfront.

1.3. Summary

- Snowflake offers a lot of flexibility to manage a complex data environment.

- A Snowflake account is deployed and associated on a specific cloud provider and region.

- We recommend using a separate Snowflake account for development, testing, and production.

CHAPTER 2

Infrastructure Security

This chapter deals with the infrastructure security behind your Snowflake account. This is mainly about things that are good to know, or important decisions to make, as opposed to things that you should take action about on an ongoing basis. We believe that it's important to also discuss the infrastructure security parts that you don't have control over, so you can understand what's happening under the hood, so you can answer questions that may arise during security assessments.

In addition to that, some topics here may influence the account plan that you choose to have on all or some of your accounts.

2.1. Account Data Storage

The answer is that when you create a Snowflake account, you choose on which public cloud and in which region your data is stored. At this time, Snowflake supports data in AWS, Azure, and GCP (Google Cloud Platform). Within the public cloud, the data is stored in storage buckets (S3 in AWS, Azure Blobs in Azure, and GCS in GCP). In any case, and whichever deployment option you choose, the storage buckets used are per account.

The data storage itself, in the physical level, is protected per the physical security policy of each public cloud provider. Over the years, we spoke with a lot of organizations doing some sort of a cloud migration, and physical security is often not a concern, and your organization probably has other assets already on a public cloud. In any case, if you want to drill down into that, you can refer to the specific public cloud provider's physical security policy and terms.

© Ben Herzberg, Yoav Cohen 2022
B. Herzberg and Y. Cohen, *Snowflake Security*, https://doi.org/10.1007/978-1-4842-7389-0_2

In most cases, obviously, organizations choose to have their Snowflake accounts in the public cloud they're using, as this makes the integration easier and more cost-effective. For example, when transferring data for ingestion, it can be within the same public cloud's region, and access to data is also done from the same public cloud. As we will see in the following, there are also options to have a tighter integration to your public cloud resources using a PrivateLink connection.

Depending on the organization, sometimes it makes sense to have multiple accounts, in two or more public clouds, when the organization uses several public clouds. In some cases, it also makes sense to have separate Snowflake accounts for different regions. This has a lot to do with the types of data you're storing in your Snowflake account, the compliance and regulation requirements you're facing, and your contractual obligations.

2.2. Access to the Stored Data

There are several deployment options for your Snowflake account, and not all of them exist on each public cloud (currently PrivateLink is only for AWS and Azure deployments). Let's discuss the differences between these. To understand this, it's important to understand that a Snowflake service runs within a VPC and consists of a load balancer, cloud services that are generic for the VPC's operation, a metadata store, and the virtual data warehouses. The latter are instances that are doing the actual work on your data and regardless of your plan are separate between accounts, and even within an account, you can use multiple virtual data warehouses.

2.2.1. The Standard Multi-tenant Deployment

In this deployment option, as displayed in Figure 2-1, access to the Snowflake VPC is only done in the application layer, encrypted over HTTPS. However, the data is not encrypted within the VPC itself. Your S3 bucket and virtual data warehouses (computing instances) are separated by account, but the metadata store, load balancing, and other cloud services are shared with the rest of the tenants in your VPC.

Obviously, this is not a show stopper for all organizations, but some organizations have different requirements. Let's understand the risks here. What this means is that if someone has access to the VPC, and is able to inspect traffic within the VPC, they may be able to intercept unencrypted data. Having this ability within a VPC is far from being trivial, of course.

Other than this risk, in some cases, this may not meet certain compliance standards, such as HIPAA.

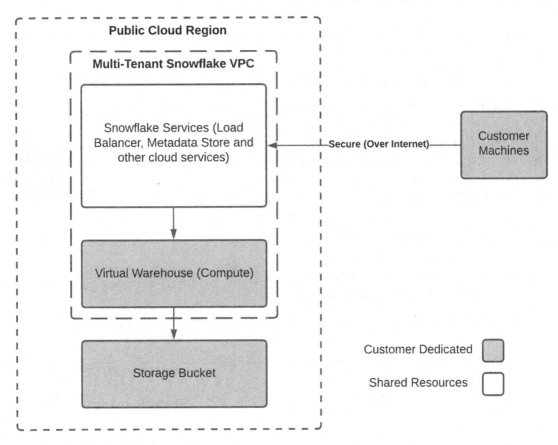

Figure 2-1. *Snowflake standard deployment*

2.2.2. Business Critical Edition

To mitigate the risks mentioned earlier, Snowflake offers a plan where data within the
VPC is also sent encrypted. Using this deployment option, you may also use the tri-secret
security feature. As you can see in Figure 2-2, though using the same multi-tenant cloud
services, the data is now encrypted by customer managed keys. For more information
about that, refer to the encryption chapter, but the main thing to remember is that this
edition allows you to have your own managed keys.

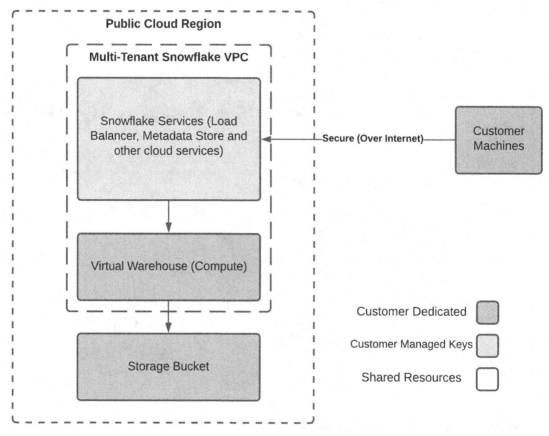

Figure 2-2. *Customer managed keys deployment*

2.2.3. Virtual Private Snowflake

Definitely not for most organizations, but if your risk or regulation compliance requirements are even higher, the next option you have is to use a Virtual Private Snowflake (VPS), which means that you are no longer part of a multi-tenant service, and the entire VPC is not shared with other Snowflake customers. You can see this dedicated customer deployment in Figure 2-3. In addition to that, you can have an egress proxy in your VPS, for added control over the traffic. Using a VPS is mostly done in heavily regulated environments such as financial institutions.

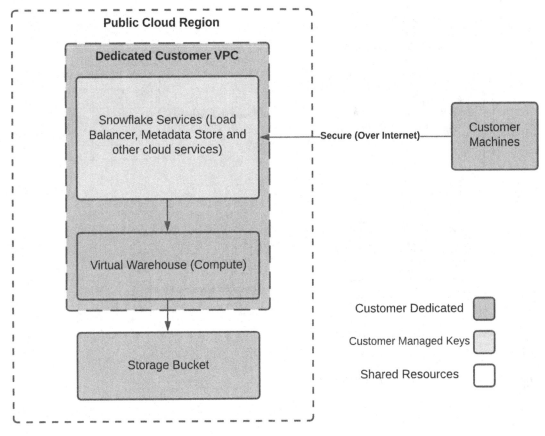

Figure 2-3. *Virtual Private Snowflake deployment*

2.2.4. PrivateLink

PrivateLink offers a direct connection from your VPC to your Snowflake deployment, without the traffic going out of your public cloud and to the Internet. You are able to connect PrivateLink to any Snowflake deployments, regardless of whether it's VPS or multi-tenant. For more information about PrivateLink, please refer to Chapter 5, "Network Access Control." In Figure 2-4, you can see a deployment of PrivateLink with customer managed keys. Note that the difference is only the connection between the customer machines and Snowflake's infrastructure, which is not done through the public Internet.

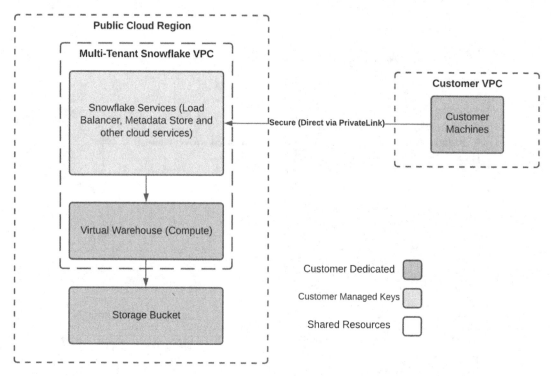

Figure 2-4. *PrivateLink architecture*

2.3. Access to Historical Data

It's important to take into account access to historical data, so you know how to balance your requirements (specifically, regarding time travel). Data that is no longer in your tables may still exist, and this may be important to know, specifically for sensitive data. For the sake of this section, when we speak of historical data, we mean data that is no longer in your current tables.

Historical data can be accessed in four different ways; let's discuss them.

2.3.1. Stage Data

Stage is where you put data that you load into Snowflake (or copy out of Snowflake). Even if data is removed from tables, it may still exist in the stage. It is important to delete stage files and stages which are no longer needed, to prevent exposure to sensitive data that's no longer needed. For more in-depth information about stage, refer to Chapter 3, "Data Encryption and Ingestion," and for information on how to monitor stage, refer to Chapter 7, "Auditing and Monitoring."

2.3.2. Internal or External Backup

Obviously, when you backup data, that is another place where you have the data. Your organization probably has backup requirements on some or all the data in your Snowflake data cloud, and it is important to be conscious about the backed up data and have clear policies about this backup, including where it's stored, who has access to it and under what conditions, how access to this backup is logged and monitored, etc.

When we refer to an "internal backup," we refer to data that is sometimes backed up within the account (to a different database, schema, or table). This is often not a good practice and can lead to data left behind, ungoverned, often containing sensitive information. Please try to make backup processes of the Snowflake data that are either contained within its existing mechanisms (time travel) or that are clear, well documented, and understood by data owners.

2.3.3. Time Travel

"Wouldn't it be great to have an UNDROP TABLE command?" Well, Snowflake has this command, as part of its time travel feature. Time travel allows you to go back in time and either undo actions (Undrop tables, schemas, and databases) or run select queries for a specific time frame.

To set up time travel, you need to change the parameter data_retention_time_in_ days for the specified object. The setting will take place for all objects sitting "under" the object. For example, if you've set the retention time to one day in a database, it will apply to all schemas and tables within the database. You can set this setting all the way up from a single table to the entire account, for example:

```
ALTER TABLE candy_flavors SET data_retention_time_in_days=30;
```

Querying historical data can be done with a SELECT query, with the *at* function or *before*. As an example, the following query will retrieve data from the candy_flavors table, as per one hour (3,600 seconds) ago:

```
SELECT * FROM candy_flavors at(offset => -3600);
```

If you want to understand more about the capabilities of time travel in Snowflake, refer to the documentation. From a security perspective, it is important to note that the ability to query data poses a challenge, mainly because of compliance reasons. For example, let's say that as a requirement coming from data protection and privacy regulation, such as the CCPA, you need to apply a process of "Right to Be Forgotten" across your data platforms, including Snowflake. The ability to pull such deleted information may be an issue, and so, in such cases, you may want to set a shorter retention period on such tables. In any case, depending on your plan, the maximum retention time may be between one day and up to 90 days. Note that setting a high value on tables with a lot of data changes may also have a large impact on your storage.

2.3.4. Fail-Safe

In addition to the "self-service restoration" that is available to you using time travel, you can also use fail-safe restoration of data by contacting Snowflake's support, for up to seven days of restoration time after the expiration of time travel. This restoration is handled by Snowflake support, and needless to say, this is an emergency cord you should avoid pulling and rely instead on more controlled methods of backup.

Note that fail-safe does not restore temporary or transient objects, and of course, these are better to be used if creating temporary objects.

2.4. Good to Know

Some things that are good to know about Snowflake's infrastructure security: As part of Snowflake's security commitment, there is no direct access to Snowflake's VPCs, and all access to the data is done through an application layer. That means that there is no engineer from Snowflake who should be able to access the buckets where your data is stored, regardless of your account plan.

In addition, your encrypted data is only decrypted in the memory of the virtual data warehouses, and only the data that needs to be decrypted for your data processing is decrypted. Furthermore, the virtual data warehouses, which are per account, are also ephemeral, meaning that they run only when needed.

It is also worth following the compliance information in Snowflake's website, but currently, Snowflake's infrastructure has compliance certification of ISO, NIST, and SOC2 for all plans and even more standards for business critical plans (PCI, HIPAA, Fedramp, and more).

2.5. Summary

In this chapter, we went through Snowflake's infrastructure security, the different deployment options, and their security and compliance differences, as well as what you need to do about backing up your infrastructure.

CHAPTER 3

Data Encryption and Ingestion

In this chapter, we'll discuss how Snowflake uses encryption to secure your data. The good news is that Snowflake already provides a high standard of built-in, out-of-the-box encryption, leaving you to decide if your use cases require anything beyond that. For most people, encryption can be confusing. Our goal for this chapter is not to teach you cryptography, but to enable you to ask the right questions and seek additional information when it becomes relevant. Use this chapter to learn what Snowflake provides and how that addresses your organization's requirements.

Encryption, in the context of a data cloud, can mean one of two things: securing the data sent to and from the data cloud, which is known as securing data in transit, and securing the data stored in tables, also known as encryption of data at rest. Both have become ubiquitous in recent years to mitigate real risks to your data.

3.1. Encryption of Data in Transit

Whenever a user queries Snowflake, the query is sent over the Internet to Snowflake, and the result set is sent back. The data passes through many networks before it reaches its destination, including your home/office network, your Internet Service Provider (ISP), sometimes a global network carrier, a public cloud network, and so on. Even when using methods like VPN (Virtual Private Network), the query still needs to get out of someone's computer and into Snowflake. With so many networks between your users and Snowflake, it's relatively easy for someone to try and leverage your data in transit, by being what is known as a man in the middle.

© Ben Herzberg, Yoav Cohen 2022
B. Herzberg and Y. Cohen, *Snowflake Security*, https://doi.org/10.1007/978-1-4842-7389-0_3

In a man-in-the-middle (MITM) attack, someone is trying to eavesdrop the data you send or receive from Snowflake, to learn your secrets or modify it without you knowing, leading you to make wrong data-driven decisions. Encryption is one of the tools used to defend against MITM attacks – by not sending clear-text data over the network, we prevent attackers from reading it, per Figure 3-1.

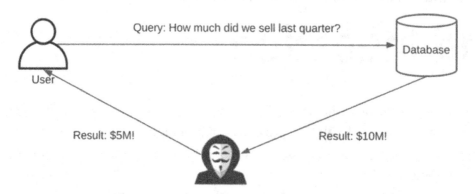

Figure 3-1. *MITM attack*

Transport Layer Security, or TLS, is the most common protocol today to encrypt data in transit. It is now known that older encryption protocols like Secure Sockets Layer (SSL) and older versions of popular encryption software like OpenSSL were vulnerable and that attackers used those vulnerabilities to steal confidential information without leaving a trace. Today, the information security community puts a lot of emphasis on ensuring the latest encryption standards are widely adopted and Snowflake follows these recommendations. In fact, like many other online services today, Snowflake encrypts all communications by default and does not accept non-encrypted communications at all.

But what happens to your data after you send it to Snowflake?

3.2. Encryption at Rest

Snowflake provides end-to-end encryption (E2EE) to ensure that only end users and the Snowflake runtime components can read your data. Even the cloud provider that your Snowflake account is deployed on cannot read your data, because the data is encrypted at rest and only decrypted in the memory of the Snowflake runtime components.

There are two main methods to load data into Snowflake. The first is by using SQL statements like INSERT or UPDATE. This method is usually reserved for smaller amounts of data, and the integrity and confidentiality of these operations is maintained by Snowflake's built-in encryption of data in transit which we discussed in the previous section. The second method is to load data by uploading files into Snowflake, and this process consists of two steps: uploading files into a staging area and copying the files into Snowflake tables. A third, optional step is unloading data from Snowflake into a file. We will analyze each step to see how the integrity and confidentiality of your data is maintained.

3.2.1. Uploading Files to Staging Areas

When uploading a data file into Snowflake, it's first uploaded to a staging area before it's copied into a table. Uploading and copying are two separate operations, and files can reside in staging areas for unlimited periods of time. Even when assuming that access to staging areas is only permitted to authenticated users, if credentials are compromised, the integrity and confidentiality of your data is at risk. Luckily, Snowflake and the cloud providers make it easy to mitigate that risk with built-in support for data encryption.

Snowflake supports two types of staging areas:

- **Snowflake-provided staging area** – Also known as an internal stage, is a Snowflake-managed file system where users can exchange files with Snowflake. Use Snowflake-managed staging areas when you need to upload files that are not yet stored in another storage bucket.

- **Customer-provided staging area** – Also known as an external stage, is a cloud file system directory, like an Amazon S3 or Google Cloud Storage bucket. Use customer-provided staging areas to upload files that are already stored on the cloud and now need to be imported into Snowflake.

3.2.2. Snowflake-Provided Staging Areas

When uploading to a Snowflake-provided staging area, Snowflake automatically encrypts the files before they are loaded into tables. Snowflake provides three types of internal staging areas:

- **User stages** – Snowflake allocates a staging area for each user. Use this option when data files should only be accessible by a single user but may be copied to multiple tables.

- **Table stages** – Snowflake allocates a staging area for each table. Use this option when data files should be accessible by multiple users but may only be copied to a single table.

- **Named stages** – These are database objects that can be created, configured, and shared, providing maximum flexibility.

For example, to upload the employees.csv file to your user staging area, use the following command:

```
PUT file:///tmp/data/employees.csv @~
```

To upload the same file to the staging area of the ORGDATA.PUBLIC.EMPLOYEES table, use

```
USE ORGDATA.PUBLIC;
PUT file:///tmp/data/employees.csv @%employees;
```

For a complete reference of the PUT statement, visit the Snowflake Documentation.

To upload a file to a named internal staging area, you will need to create it first using the CREATE STAGE statement, for example:

```
CREATE STAGE employees
```

To upload the employees.csv file to the employees' staging area we just created, use

```
PUT file:///tmp/data/employees.csv @employees
```

Internal stages provide many options which are not covered here. For a full reference, please visit the Snowflake Documentation.

Note that the preceding examples of using PUT commands are for scripting, and do not work directly from the UI worksheets. If you are using the UI to load data into Snowflake, you should use the Load Data action, within the database management, per Figure 3-2.

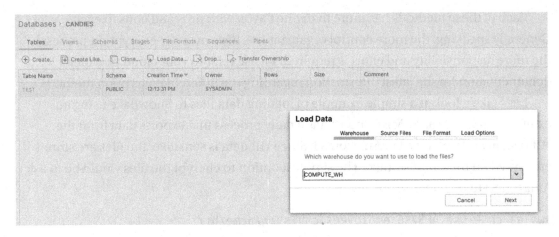

Figure 3-2. *Loading data using the Snowflake UI*

3.2.3. Customer-Provided Staging Areas

When uploading files to customer-provided or external stages, it's up to you to decide if the files should be encrypted, which we obviously recommend. Snowflake interfaces with the native capabilities of the cloud provider's storage service to manage the decryption of the files in order to copy the data to tables or the encryption process when data from tables is copied to files. While each cloud provider has a tad different set of capabilities, the following options are generally available:

1. **No encryption** – Data is sent from the client and stored in clear text on disk in the cloud provider's data center. While easiest to use, we do not recommend you use this option.

2. **Server-side encryption** – Data is sent from the client to the cloud provider and encrypted by the cloud provider before it's stored on disk. This is a good option that balances between operational overhead and security. The heavy lifting of managing encryption is off-loaded to the cloud provider, but data is stored encrypted.

3. **Client-side encryption** – Data is encrypted on the client before it's uploaded to the cloud. This is the most secure option, as clear-text data is not sent to the cloud but requires more planning and effort to operate on the customer side.

Each of these methods has more than one flavor, with pros and cons to each. Generally speaking, the more control organizations have over the encryption process, the more responsibility and effort is required. Please refer to your cloud provider's documentation for the latest information regarding the different encryption methods.

Let's take a look at a simple example of loading data files to Snowflake using an external staging area. ACME Candies has a daily process that exports data from the HR system and uploads it to Amazon S3. Since HR data is sensitive, the files are stored encrypted on the cloud storage. The simplest option to encrypt the files would be to ask Amazon S3 to do it for us:

```
aws s3 cp --sse AES256 employees.csv s3://acme/hr/
```

By using the SSE (server-side encryption) parameter, we ask Amazon S3 to generate the necessary keys to encrypt the data before it's stored on disk. To configure Snowflake to read files from this S3 bucket, we need to create an external stage, specifying AWS_SSE_S3 in the encryption options, as follows:

```
CREATE STAGE hrdata
  url='s3://acme/hr/'
  credentials=(aws_key_id='<KEY_ID>' aws_secret_key='<SECRET_KEY>')
  encryption=(type = 'AWS_SSE_S3');
```

For a full reference, please visit the Snowflake Documentation.

Note   When uploading files to customer-provided staging areas, you use the cloud provider's native tools instead of the PUT command which is reserved for Snowflake-provided staging areas. Under the hood, PUT uses the cloud provider's libraries to upload files.

Now that Snowflake has the information it needs to read your files from a staging area, let's see how your data stays secure when it's copied into Snowflake tables.

3.2.4. Using Storage Integration

A better way to connect to external storage, instead of explicitly including credentials, such as in the previous listing, is to create a storage integration between Snowflake and the public cloud in which the storage for the external stage is located. This has the following security benefits:

- You do not have to transfer credentials within the queries when performing CREATE STAGE.

- You can specify specific locations for your stages explicitly to have better control of where data is loaded from and into.

To set up a storage integration, you should follow the Snowflake documentation at `https://docs.snowflake.com/en/user-guide/data-load-s3-config-storage-integration.html`, and here are some security considerations when setting up security integrations.

An important consideration is that if the data files are managed by a process external to Snowflake, you should set a read-only policy, so that you lower the risk of a Snowflake user exporting data to these buckets.

In order to reduce risks of sensitive data exposure in loading and unloading of data, using integration with the storage allows you to set the external stage availability and then allow the roles who can create stages to stay within these boundaries.

3.2.5. How Snowflake Encrypts Your Data in Tables

Once data files are uploaded to a staging area, Snowflake can read them and copy the data into tables. For example, to copy the employees.csv file from the external stage we just created, use the COPY INTO statement:

```
COPY INTO employees FROM @hrdata/employees.csv;
```

For a full reference, please visit the Snowflake Documentation.

A table is stored in one or more files, which Snowflake stores using the storage service of the cloud provider. Table files are automatically encrypted by Snowflake, with each file encrypted using a different data encryption key, to limit the scope of data each key controls. With so many tables and files, each encrypted using a different key, managing all these keys can become very complex. To simplify this process, Snowflake uses a technique called key wrapping, or envelope encryption.

In key wrapping (per Figure 3-3), the key used to encrypt a file is stored alongside the file. To protect the data encryption key, it's stored in encrypted form, using a higher-level key that is kept secret. When the file needs to be decrypted, the data encryption key is extracted from the file and decrypted using the higher-level key, and then it can be used to decrypt the contents of the file. Key wrapping removes the need to store all of the encryption keys in clear text in a secure location, like a key management service. Instead, only the higher-level key is stored in a secure location.

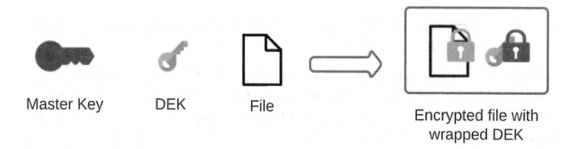

Figure 3-3. *Key wrapping*

Snowflake Hierarchical Key Model

Snowflake also uses a form of key wrapping to manage how table files are encrypted. Keys are organized in a hierarchical model which includes the following levels, as shown in Figure 3-4:

1. **File keys** – Used to encrypt and decrypt individual table files. File keys are stored, encrypted, alongside the files.

2. **Table master keys** – Used to encrypt and decrypt the file keys. Table master keys are stored, encrypted, in the table's metadata.

3. **Account master keys** – Used to encrypt and decrypt the table master keys. Account master keys are stored, encrypted, in the account's metadata.

4. **Root keys** – Used to encrypt and decrypt the account master keys. Root keys only reside in a hardware security module (HSM) and are never extracted from it. All cryptographic operations are performed inside the HSM. For example, when an account

master key is loaded from the account metadata and needs to be decrypted, it is sent to the HSM to be decrypted using the root key rather than extracting the root key from the HSM to perform that task. The root key is the only key that is stored in clear text which is why it never leaves the HSM.

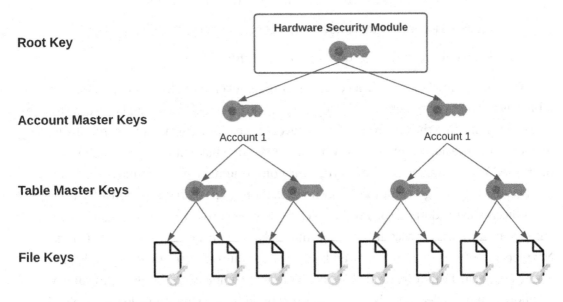

Figure 3-4. *Snowflake hierarchical key model*

Note   Hardware security modules are physical devices that are used to securely store secret information, such as passwords or encryption keys, and to perform cryptographic operations using them. HSMs are built according to strict standards to be tamper resistant, to prevent theft of information and in some cases will erase the data they hold to avoid it getting leaked. They are the gold standard when it comes to storing sensitive data securely. All cloud providers offer HSM services.

The process to encrypt new data is as follows:

1. The user executes a COPY INTO statement to copy data from a staging area to a table.

2. Snowflake creates a new file key and uses it to encrypt the new data file.

3. Snowflake uses the table key to encrypt the file key and stores it alongside the file.

4. The encrypted file and data key are stored together.

The process of decrypting data, for example, when the table is queried, is as follows:

1. Snowflake extracts the encrypted file key from the data file.

2. Snowflake uses the table key to decrypt the file key.

3. Snowflake uses the file key to decrypt the file.

Whenever Snowflake needs a key from a higher level of the hierarchy, for example, a table key to encrypt or decrypt a file key, it needs to load the encrypted key from storage and decrypt it using the key from the next level of the hierarchy, which eventually leads to decrypting the account master key in the HSM. Snowflake maintains a cache of decrypted keys in the memory of its runtime components to ensure this process is fast.

Because keys can get compromised, Snowflake constrains both the amount of data each key protects and the duration of time in which the key can be used to read the data. Snowflake automatically rotates the account and table master keys when they are more than 30 days old. New versions of the keys are created, and older versions are only used to decrypt older data.

To complete the life cycle and phase out older keys completely, Snowflake provides an additional feature called periodic rekeying. When periodic rekeying is enabled, table files that were encrypted with keys that were retired over a year ago are automatically re-encrypted using new keys. The new keys will be used to decrypt the files from now on. Periodic rekeying also ensures that older data is re-encrypted using the latest security standards and technology.

3.2.6. Unloading Files to Staging Areas

Data can not only be copied from a file to a Snowflake table; the opposite direction is possible as well. Unloading data, which is the process of copying data from a Snowflake table to a file, is useful when you have to export data from Snowflake to another system. Snowflake handles the encryption of data you unload in much the same way as for loading data: when data is unloaded into a Snowflake-managed, or internal, staging area, Snowflake automatically encrypts the files and decrypts them for you when you download them using the GET statement. For example, use the following to export the employees table to a CSV file:

```
GET @%employees file:///tmp/data/employees.csv
```

When data is unloaded to a customer-provided, or external, staging area, Snowflake would use the specified encryption option in the stage's definition to encrypt the files. For example:

```
COPY INTO @hrdata/employees-out.csv FROM employees
```

When you download the files from the external stage, they will be decrypted by the cloud provider's SDK.

Using the hierarchical key model, Snowflake offers a comprehensive solution to securing your data at rest using encryption. It also ensures that data coming in and out of Snowflake is encrypted as well.

3.2.7. External Tables

You can not only import data to tables within Snowflake, but can also access files located in external stages by creating an external table that is mapped to that file, by using the CREATE EXTERNAL TABLE command. These tables will be read-only, as well as slower than regular tables, and will be typically used in situations like data-lake querying, or as part of an ingestion process where the raw data is processed from these tables. In many cases, it makes sense to add secure views for querying the data from external tables, to create an abstraction layer between the users and the raw data.

From a security perspective, it is important to remember that these files are placed in public cloud buckets, and (especially when they contain sensitive data) you should make sure that access to the files is also limited and monitored in the public cloud. For more information about external tables, refer to the Snowflake documentation.

3.2.8. Customer Managed Keys

For organizations that need more control over the keys used to secure their data in Snowflake, Snowflake provides an additional feature called Tri-Secret Secure, which integrates customer-owned keys into Snowflake's key hierarchy.

In Tri-Secret Secure, as per Figure 3-5, customers generate their own root key using the cloud provider's key management service and allow Snowflake to access it. Snowflake uses both the customer-generated root key and the Snowflake-generated root key to create a composed account master key. Now, when Snowflake needs to unwrap the composed account master key, it needs to access both its HSM and the customer-controlled KMS.

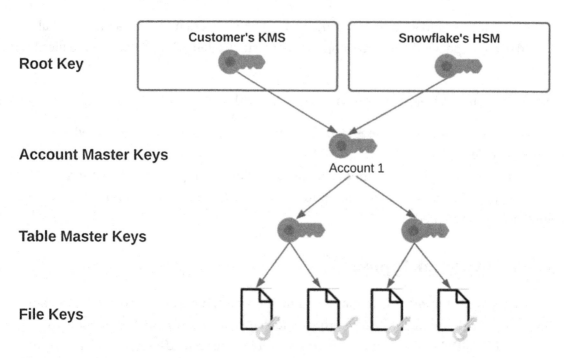

Figure 3-5. *Tri-Secret Secure*

With Tri-Secret Secure, your data in Snowflake cannot be decrypted without your approval to access the root key in your KMS. This also means that in the case of a data breach, you can block Snowflake from decrypting any data and thus stopping any data processing activity in your Snowflake account. However, as mentioned before, whenever you are responsible for encryption keys, you need to make sure that your organization is willing to accept the challenge of keeping them safe and available. Failure to meet that challenge will result in data loss.

3.2.9. Application-Level Encryption

In all the encryption methods we discussed, Snowflake has access to the keys it needs to decrypt your data, whether they are customer or Snowflake generated. In the event of compromised keys, there's risk to at least some of your data.

Another approach to gain even more control over how your data is encrypted is not to share keys with Snowflake at all. Application-level encryption is a form of client-side encryption; however, decryption keys are not shared in advance with the server side, if they are shared at all. In application-level encryption, the user encrypts the data before it's loaded to Snowflake, and the data is stored in Snowflake tables in encrypted form. For this to work, the client has to encrypt the data at the field level and not the file level. From Snowflake's perspective, it doesn't even know that data is encrypted.

For example, let's assume that the HR department collects the latest manager's review on each employee and stores it as text in the "review" column in the employees table. ACME's policy is to keep this data as secure as possible – even in the event of a compromised encryption key. ACME encrypts the column before it loads data to Snowflake, so the review text is stored in encrypted form in Snowflake tables. Even if any of the keys in Snowflake's hierarchical key mode is compromised, attackers can potentially decrypt the employees table, but not the review text.

The downside of using application-level encryption is that it makes it harder to use your data in Snowflake. For example, if the HR manager wants to list all employees that received raving reviews from their manager by looking up specific keywords in the comment text, Snowflake won't be able to find those, because the comment text is encrypted. For example, the following query would not return any results:

```
SELECT id, first_name, last_name
FROM employees
WHERE review ILIKE '%incredible%'
```

There are a few ways to work around this challenge. The first one is to process the data in multiple steps: list all employees, potentially unloading the entire table to a file and then decrypting the comment text before analyzing the data locally. We don't recommend this approach because it is cumbersome and creates copies of your data (one in Snowflake, one in the staging area, and one in your local computer) which ends up increasing the risk of a data breach.

A second option is to use Snowflake's built-in decryption function as part of processing the query. Let's assume that we encrypted the comment text in the review column using a passphrase, by either Snowflake's built-in ENCRYPT function or a compatible implementation. The same query shown earlier can now be rewritten to tell Snowflake to decrypt the review column only when we query it:

```
SELECT id, first_name, last_name
FROM employees
WHERE DECRYPT(review, '<PASSPHRASE>') ILIKE '%incredible%'
```

As part of processing this query, Snowflake would call the decrypt function on the comment text stored in the review column and would only return rows with the word incredible in the comment text.

A third option, similar to the second one, is to use external user-defined functions (UDF) to perform the decryption by a third-party service that customers control. You can define an external UDF that calls your service to decrypt the data, for example:

```
CREATE OR REPLACE EXTERNAL FUNCTION decrypt_varchar_ext(v varchar)
 varchar api_integration = acme_api1 AS '<AWS API GW URL>';
```

And then use the UDF in the same way as Snowflake's built-in DECRYPT function:

```
SELECT id, first_name, last_name
FROM employees
WHERE decrypt_varchar_ext(review) ILIKE '%incredible%'
```

However, in both the built-in decryption function and the external UDF, clear-text data will be processed by Snowflake as part of processing the query. The only way to avoid sharing clear-text data with Snowflake is to encrypt it at the field level before it is loaded, but as discussed already, controlling the encryption and decryption processes puts more responsibility on you to make sure your data is kept available and safe. We recommend considering application-level encryption only for a small number of specific fields and to spend time understanding the consequences of using this method.

Note that the function mentioned before may as well not decrypt payloads, but de-tokenize it using an external function. That means that the field will contain a token (identifier) which, in certain cases, will call an external function that retrieves the value for the token. For example, the function has a key-value solution that transforms tokens to payment card information, only in specific cases.

Note   Homomorphic encryption is a field of cryptography that deals with running computations on encrypted data without decrypting it. We are seeing some encouraging early results of using homomorphic encryption in data stores and expect to see more of that in the future.

3.3. Summary

- Snowflake takes care of securing your data when it's sent or received to or from Snowflake.

- When you want to load data into Snowflake from a cloud storage bucket you own, it's up to you to encrypt the data you put there and configure Snowflake so it can read it to copy it into tables.

- Snowflake uses a form of key wrapping to encrypt your tables and manages encryption keys in a hierarchical model, encrypting each file with its own key.

- Snowflake enables customers to bring their own keys (BYOK) into the key hierarchy for greater control over the encryption process.

- Application-level encryption can be utilized to protect highly sensitive data at the field level without handing over keys to Snowflake.

- The more control you take over the encryption process, the more responsibilities you take on for keeping it secure and available.

CHAPTER 4

Authentication: Keeping Strangers Out

Not everybody can enter ACME Candies' offices. There is a certain process of who is allowed to enter and under which conditions:

- Employees can get inside the office by using their personal RFID badges.

- Employees from other branches can get inside the office, but only after they show their employee badge to the receptionist, which calls their company cellular number to verify.

- Partners or guests have to be accompanied by an employee.

In the same way you wouldn't want strangers to roam around your office (especially if you're working from home), you definitely don't want strangers to roam around your data. This can have dire consequences, and this is why it's important to have a very clear and effective authentication policy. In this chapter, we will discuss authentication to your Snowflake data cloud. We will take a look at the different authentication features Snowflake offers and discuss their pros and cons.

4.1. Users Management

Snowflake users can either be created manually in Snowflake or provisioned automatically by an identity provider, such as Okta or Azure AD. We recommend the latter whenever possible to both simplify user onboarding and ensure users are removed if they are no longer needed.

© Ben Herzberg, Yoav Cohen 2022
B. Herzberg and Y. Cohen, *Snowflake Security*, https://doi.org/10.1007/978-1-4842-7389-0_4

Creating local Snowflake users is done either by using the Web UI of Snowflake or by using the CREATE USER command:

```
CREATE [ OR REPLACE ] USER [ IF NOT EXISTS ] <name>
  [ objectProperties ]
  [ objectParams ]
  [ sessionParams ]
```

For the complete list of parameters, you can refer to the Snowflake Documentation. This can be as simple as

```
CREATE USER testuser PASSWORD='abc';
```

Though simple, this is a great example of Snowflake giving us a lot of flexibility which can also drive us to dark places (in terms of security). The password parameter has no policy enforcement over it and can literally be "abc" like in the earlier example. Using such simple passwords is like keeping the engine going in a brand new car while going out for milk.

> *In the Authentication world, we call different types of authentication methods "factors." Each factor is a specific type of credential used to verify the identity of a user or an application. A long time ago, not all systems and services used any authentication factor. In some legacy systems, there are still no authentication factors, but in most, there is at least one factor of authentication (such as a user/password combination, a PIN code, a private-public key pair, etc.).*

Nowadays, for human-based authentication, to reduce risks of account takeover attacks, it is recommended to use two-factor authentication (or in short 2FA). Note that by requiring two factors, we require a different type of credential, so it is not another password (also known as "something you know"), but rather, in most cases some sort of a token provided by an authenticator application ("something you have"). That token is often referred to as a one-time password (or OTP). Now, even if your password is compromised, the attacker will not be able to access your account, as they don't have the OTP required in addition to the password.

Moreover, as we will discuss in this chapter, configuring users with passwords as a sole means of authentication is not a good practice. Passwords get leaked, reused, or are otherwise a "sitting target" for attackers. Using Snowflake users with passwords is best to be avoided, in favor of other means of authentication, but when it *is* used, the risks it poses should be negated by adding different ways of security.

4.2. User Provisioning

User provisioning means that the actions around users' creation, modification, or removal of user accounts are handled from a centralized place. There can be different identity data sources in organizations (e.g., HR systems, CRM, and user directories).

User provisioning allows for operational efficiency when onboarding users, modifying users' roles within organizations, etc. It is also an important part of meeting compliance requirements and maintaining an effective security posture for an organization.

Snowflake supports several ways of integrating with identity management platforms or identity providers (IdP)/identity management (IDM) platforms such as Okta, Azure AD, and others. By completing this integration, the authentication of users will be done by using a Single Sign-On (SSO) process, and not by issuing separate credentials for Snowflake. This is a better security choice, as it will enforce the authentication policy set by your organization, such as two-factor authentication, password strength, etc. It will also remove another place where your users' passwords are stored. Lastly, from an end-user perspective, they get a uniform experience across all corporate applications.

4.2.1. SCIM Integration

SCIM, which stands for *System for Cross-domain Identity Management*, is a standard whose current version (SCIM 2) was released by IETF (Internet Engineering Task Force) in 2015. SCIM is using a RESTful API for managing identity across different platforms.

The principles of setting up SCIM in Snowflake, regardless of the specific integration you're using, are that you create a security integration of SCIM type and assign a role to it. You then generate the API access token using Snowflake and use it in your SCIM application.

Okta Integration

Okta is a popular identity management platform and is very simple to integrate. In Okta, you define groups for the users in organizations (or inherit them from other directories, like LDAP). When integrating Okta with Snowflake, you can use it for the following provisioning.

User Management

You can use the Okta integration for creating, modifying, or deleting Okta users in Snowflake. That way, as an example, when a new employee is onboarded, they will automatically have a Snowflake user account created for them.

Role Management

We will learn more about role management and data authorization in later chapters, but know that the integration allows you to push your Okta groups to Snowflake, which will create a role for each Okta group, and also grant the members of the Okta groups with those roles.

In other words, when you have a team in Okta, called "Marketing Ops," which has five members, with SCIM integration, you can set them up in Okta and not need to create them (or modify them). You will, however, need to define within Snowflake what the MARKETINGOPS role will allow them to do. In summary, you can only map Okta groups to Snowflake roles.

Security Considerations

By default, Okta users are created, and a random password is generated for them in Snowflake. We recommend disabling this, so that users will only be able to access Snowflake using Okta's SSO authentication. The security reasoning is that the more authentication options you give, the more chances there are that things can go wrong. If users **should** only log in to your Snowflake using Okta SSO, enforce it.

To do that, edit the Snowflake integration in Okta, and under **Sync Password**, uncheck the setting **Generate a new random password whenever the user's Okta password changes**.

For more information about Okta SCIM integration, refer to the Snowflake documentation at `https://docs.snowflake.com/en/user-guide/scim-okta.html`.

ACME Candies Wants This!

You, master of all things data in ACME Candies, checked and found out that until now ACME Candies was using only "local" Snowflake users. You understand that this adds risks to the authentication process and creates overhead when managing users, so you want to integrate Snowflake with Okta. Here's what you need to do:

1. If you do not have an Okta account and would just like to experiment, you can open a free 30-day trial account here: www.okta.com/free-trial/.

   This will take you through the process of creating an account and setting up multifactor authentication.

2. In Okta, once logged in, go to ***Directory ➤ Groups***, and click ***Add Group***.

3. Give this group a name per the example in Figure 4-1, and click ***Add Group*** within the dialog window.

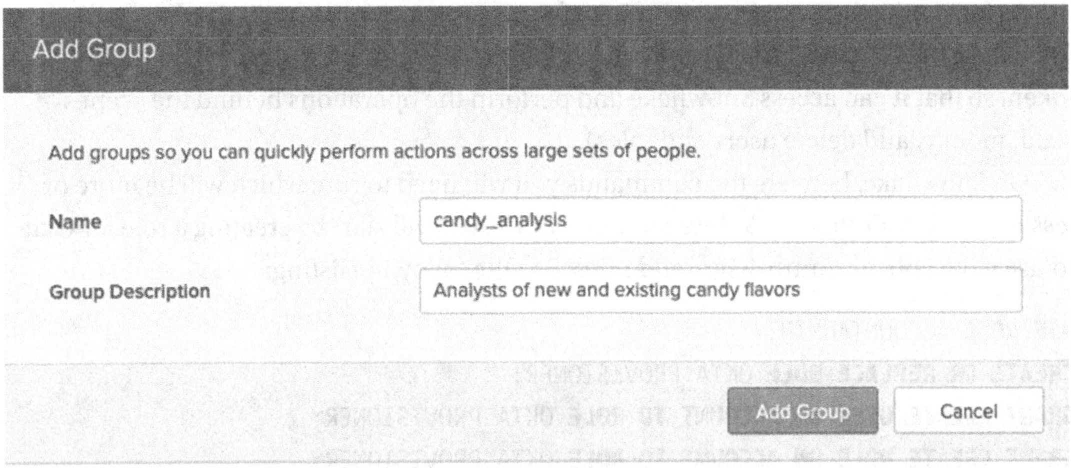

Figure 4-1. *Adding a new Okta group*

4. Go to ***Directory ➤ People***, and add a user per the following example, and click ***Add User***.

5. Go to ***Applications ➤ Create New App***, and choose the Snowflake integration, and click the ***Add*** button.

6. In the next screen, fill your Snowflake account identifier (e.g., if your account URL is https://acme.snowflakecomputing.com, enter acmeindustries). If the account name also includes a region (e.g., if your account URL is https://acme.us-east-1.snowflakecomputing.com), the identifier should include the region as well.

At this point, you will be asked about the authentication method you'd like to use. You should use SAML 2.0 (Security Assertion Markup Language) as the authentication method. In essence, integrating SSO ensures that your organization's authentication policy is enforced across the organization, including multifactor authentication. For more information on why this is recommended, see the SAML 2.0 section later.

To do that, click the ***View Setup Instructions*** button, which will open a new window with a SQL command configuring the security integration in Snowflake. Note that this query needs to be run in the ACCOUNTADMIN role. This step configures Okta as a security integration in Snowflake and tells Snowflake how to authenticate login requests (using the provided certificate in the "certificate" parameter) and where to redirect unauthenticated users to (using the "ssoUrl" parameter).

As for setting the actual provisioning of users and groups, you will need to "tell" Snowflake how to trust Okta for provisioning users and groups and give Okta an API token, so that it can access Snowflake and perform the operations behind the scenes (add, modify, and delete users and roles).

On Snowflake, here are the commands you will need to run, which will be more or less the same for other SCIM integrations as well. We will start by creating a role for Okta to use to be able to control users and roles. See the following listing:

```
USE ROLE ACCOUNTADMIN;
CREATE OR REPLACE ROLE OKTA_PROVISIONER;
GRANT CREATE USER ON ACCOUNT TO ROLE OKTA_PROVISIONER;
GRANT CREATE ROLE ON ACCOUNT TO ROLE OKTA_PROVISIONER;
GRANT ROLE okta_provisioner TO ROLE ACCOUNTADMIN;
```

We continue by creating the actual security integration. This is the setting that tells Snowflake that it allows Okta to provision users and roles using SCIM API:

```
CREATE OR REPLACE SECURITY INTEGRATION okta_provisioning
TYPE = scim
SCIM_CLIENT = 'okta'
RUN_AS_ROLE = 'OKTA_PROVISIONER';
```

Now that Snowflake is configured to accept SCIM API commands from Okta, we need to fetch the API token from Snowflake and configure Okta. You generate the token with the following command:

```
SELECT system$generate_scim_access_token('okta_provisioning');
```

Copy the token, and head to Okta, where under the Snowflake application configuration, you should navigate to **Provisioning** and choose the **Integration** sub-menu. Make sure that the "Enable API Integration" checkbox is checked, and paste the token. You can now hit the **Test API Credentials** button to make sure the integration now works.

In the **Assignments** menu, you will be able to assign users and groups to Snowflake, and these are the configurations which will be set in Snowflake (see Figure 4-2). The users will be set as Snowflake users, and the groups will be set as Snowflake roles. Furthermore, each user will be granted with the roles of the groups they are assigned to. This will, of course, still leave you with configuring access for the different roles, which we will discuss in Chapter 5, "Network Access Control."

Figure 4-2. *Integration screen in Okta*

As you can see in the previous listing, the permissions we've given the OKTA_ PROVISIONER role, and thus to the Okta user, are very broad and allow it to create and manage users and roles. It is advised to set a network policy over the SCIM integration with Okta. For more information about that, read section "Assigning a Network Policy Over SCIM."

Azure Active Directory Integration

In the same way that you can add an Okta built-in integration, Snowflake also supports a built-in integration with Azure AD. The decision of which integration to use will depend on the identity management platform that your organization uses. If you are using Azure AD as an IdP, you can set up user and groups provisioning for Snowflake, and conceptually the process is done in the same way – configuring Snowflake to create a token for the SCIM API calls and then setting up provisioning in Azure AD.

If you do not have an Azure account but would like to still experiment, you can sign up for a one-year free trial, though in most cases you want to set up user provisioning if your organization already uses Azure AD.

Setting Up the Integration in Snowflake

To set up the integration in Snowflake, you will need to set up the user and role to be used as the provisioner, which is pretty similar to the way we do this in Okta or other SCIM integrations:

```
USE ROLE accountadmin;
CREATE OR REPLACE ROLE aad_provisioner;
GRANT CREATE USER ON ACCOUNT TO ROLE aad_provisioner;
GRANT CREATE ROLE ON ACCOUNT TO ROLE aad_provisioner;
GRANT ROLE aad_provisioner TO ROLE accountadmin;
CREATE OR REPLACE SECURITY INTEGRATION aad_provisioning
    type = scim
    scim_client = 'azure'
    run_as_role = 'AAD_PROVISIONER';
```

Now, we generate and copy the authentication token for the SCIM API calls; you will need it for the Azure portal setup:

```
SELECT system$generate_scim_access_token('AAD_PROVISIONING');
```

Setting Up the Integration in Azure

To set up integration in Azure, go to your Azure portal, and in there, go to **Azure Active Directory**. Once inside, head to **Enterprise Applications**, and click the **New Application** button (as per Figure 4-3). This will take you to the Azure AD gallery page, which shows you the applications you can add to your Azure AD, in which you should search for **Snowflake AAD**, and then select it (per Figure 4-4).

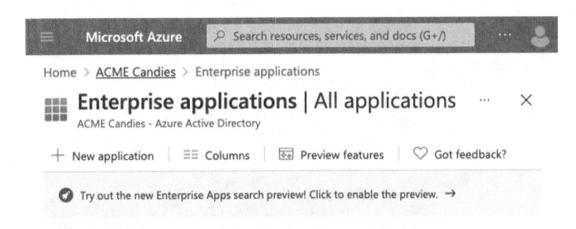

Figure 4-3. *The Enterprise applications screen*

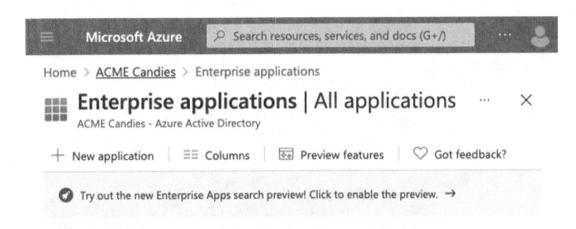

Figure 4-4. *Searching for Snowflake in Azure AD Gallery*

In the next screen, choose a name for the Snowflake integration, per Figure 4-5.

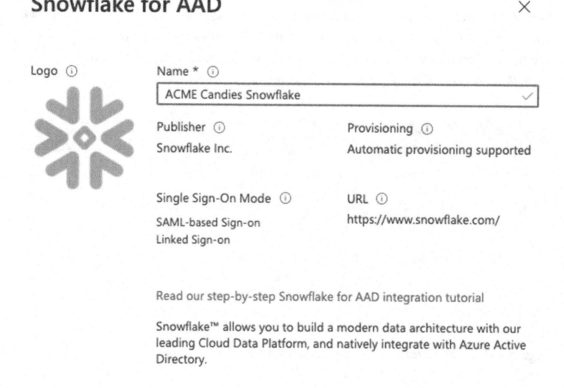

Figure 4-5. *Choosing a name for the Snowflake integration*

Once you create the integration, you will be redirected to the Snowflake AAD application dashboard. In this page, first assign the users and groups for the Snowflake AAD. The users are assigned both for provisioning and (if you choose to, which we highly recommend) for SSO. Note that not in all Azure subscription plans you will be able to assign groups, and for that, you might need to set up a trial period. You are adding users by clicking the Add user/group button in the Users and groups screen, as per Figure 4-6.

Figure 4-6. *Users and groups*

Once you've assigned the users to Snowflake, go to the ***Provision Users and Groups***, and hit the ***Get Started*** button. In the following settings screen, fill in the following information:

- Provisioning mode – Automatic

- Tenant URL – https://<YOUR ACCOUNT>.snowflakecomputing. com/scim/v2/

Under ***Secret Token***, put the token you got from the ***generate_scim_access_token*** command in Snowflake (in the earlier section "Setting Up the Integration in Snowflake"). The results should look like Figure 4-7. You will then need to save the settings and then start provisioning from the Provisioning page (per Figure 4-8) which you can reach from the navigation menu. Provisioning may take a couple of minutes, and you can see the status in the ***Snowflake AAD Application*** screen, but you now have provisioning configured.

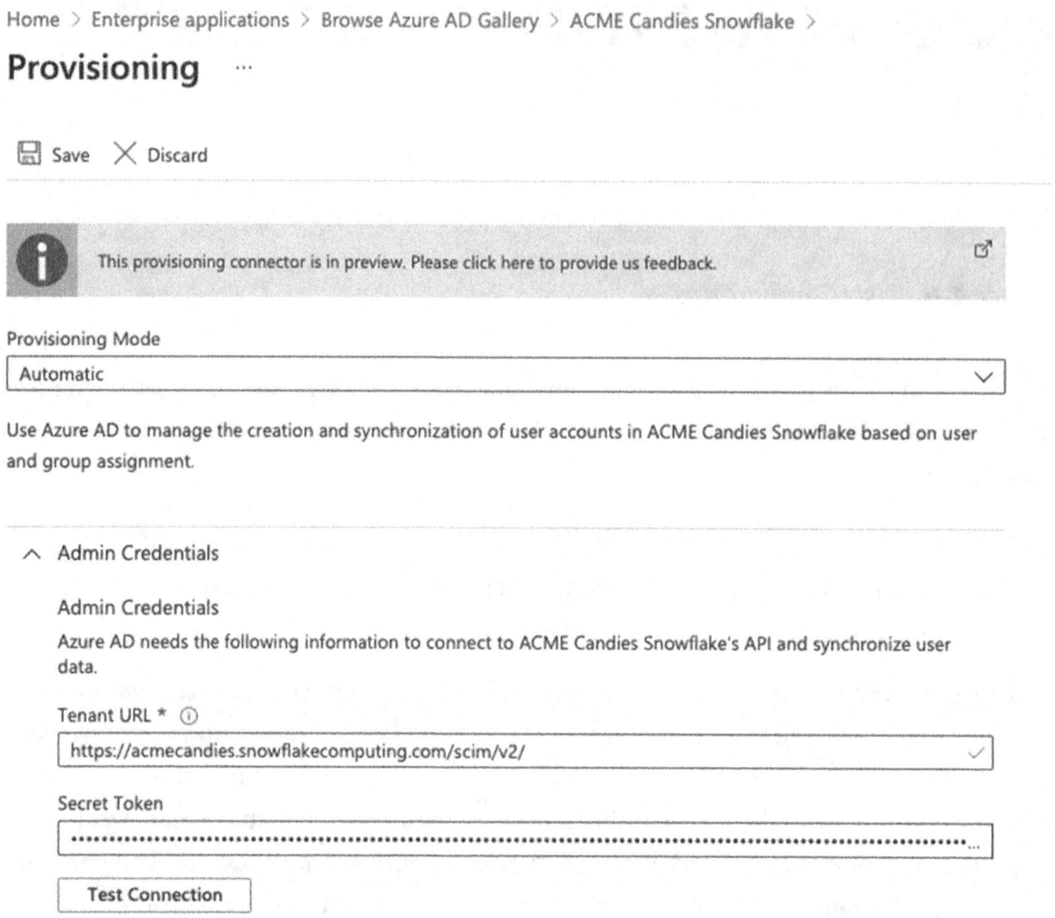

Home > Enterprise applications > Browse Azure AD Gallery > ACME Candies Snowflake >

Provisioning   ...

🖫 Save   ✕ Discard

ⓘ   This provisioning connector is in preview. Please click here to provide us feedback.   ⬈

Provisioning Mode

Automatic	⌄

Use Azure AD to manage the creation and synchronization of user accounts in ACME Candies Snowflake based on user and group assignment.

∧   Admin Credentials

Admin Credentials

Azure AD needs the following information to connect to ACME Candies Snowflake's API and synchronize user data.

Tenant URL * ⓘ

https://acmecandies.snowflakecomputing.com/scim/v2/	✓

Secret Token

•••...

Test Connection

Figure 4-7.   *Setting up provisioning*

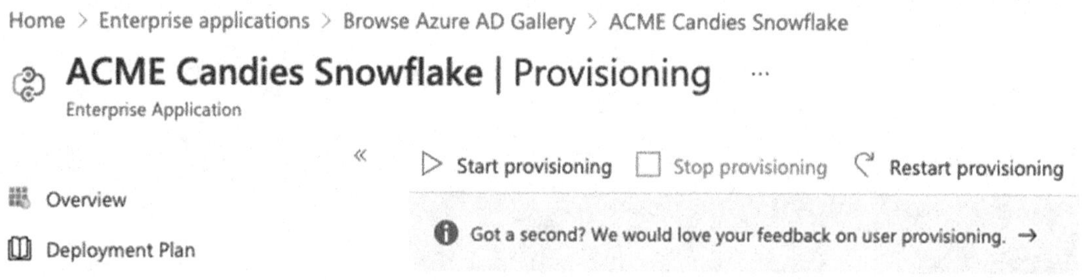

Home > Enterprise applications > Browse Azure AD Gallery > ACME Candies Snowflake

🕸 **ACME Candies Snowflake | Provisioning**   ...
Enterprise Application

《   ▷ Start provisioning   ☐ Stop provisioning   ↺ Restart provisioning

🏭 Overview

📖 Deployment Plan   ⓘ   Got a second? We would love your feedback on user provisioning. →

Figure 4-8.   *Starting the actual provisioning*

As with Okta SCIM integration, because the provisioning is using a role that enables very strong changes to your data access (managing users and roles), we recommend setting a network access policy on the Azure SCIM integration as well, to add an additional layer of security. See section "Assigning a Network Policy Over SCIM" for more details.

Other SCIM

At the time of writing, the two supported identity management integrations are Okta and Azure AD, but you can manually configure SCIM for other identity management platforms, or even for creating a custom application that provisions Snowflake users and roles using the SCIM protocol.

The principles are the same – you create a security integration of SCIM type and assign a role to it. You then generate the API access token using Snowflake and use it in your custom application. As an example, let's create a sample SCIM integration, by running the following SQL commands for creating the provisioning role and the integration:

```
CREATE OR REPLACE ROLE SELFSERVICE_PROVISIONER;
GRANT CREATE USER ON ACCOUNT TO ROLE SELFSERVICE_PROVISIONER;
GRANT CREATE ROLE ON ACCOUNT TO ROLE SELFSERVICE_PROVISIONER;
GRANT ROLE SELFSERVICE_PROVISIONER TO ROLE ACCOUNTADMIN;

CREATE OR REPLACE SECURITY INTEGRATION SELFSERVICE_PROVISIONING
    TYPE = scim
    SCIM_CLIENT = 'generic'
    RUN_AS_ROLE = 'SELFSERVICE_PROVISIONER';
```

Now that the integration is active, we need to generate an API access token:

```
SELECT system$generate_scim_access_token('SELFSERVICE_PROVISIONING');
```

Taking the generated access token, we can then integrate into our application, when sending REST API calls; as an example, the following curl command will use our token to generate a new test user. Obviously, you will need to adjust it for your needs:

```
curl --location --request POST 'https://acme.snowflakecomputing.com/scim/
v2/Users' \
--header 'Authorization: Bearer <YOURTOKEN>' \
```

```
--header 'Content-Type: application/scim+json' \
--header 'Accept-Encoding: utf-8' \
--header 'Accept-Charset: utf-8' \
--data-raw '{
"schemas": [
"urn:ietf:params:scim:schemas:core:2.0:User",
"urn:ietf:params:scim:schemas:extension:enterprise:2.0:User"
],
"userName": "user1",
"password": "some_password",
"name": {
"givenName": "willy",
"familyName": "wonka"
},
"emails": [
{
"value": "willy.w@acme.com"
}
],
"displayName": "WillyW",
"active": true
}'
```

You can find examples of the rest of the REST API calls here: https://documenter. getpostman.com/view/5462540/S1Lzx6gY?version=latest#intro.

Assigning a Network Policy over SCIM

User and role provisioning, as we've seen, is using a generated API token for actions which are very powerful (enabling people to access data). Unless you specifically configure the integration to work with a network policy, the SCIM API calls can be sent from any source network. That is why we recommend that you assign a network policy to allow SCIM calls to only be sent from the identity management platforms.

To do that, we need to define a network policy that will allow access only from specific IP addresses and then apply this policy on the SCIM integration. Creating the network policy should be based on the IP addresses used by the identity management provider (e.g., you can find Okta's IP addresses here: `https://s3.amazonaws.com/ okta-ip-ranges/ip_ranges.json`), and you can create the policy with the CREATE NETWORK POLICY command (read more on network policies in Chapter 5, "Network Access Control").

Once the network policy is configured, use the following command to apply the network access limitation on the SCIM integration:

```
ALTER SECURITY INTEGRATION okta_provisioning
SET network_policy = <name_of_the_network_policy>;
```

SCIM Token Management

As with other secrets, it is a good practice to rotate the API token for SCIM integration. This reduces risks of token misuse and may also be mandated by compliance auditing. To generate a new token, simply rerun the ***CREATE OR REPLACE SECURITY INTEGRATION*** command, and generate a new token. Our recommendation is, depending on your size of operation, perform this once every three to six months.

Obviously, this process can be scripted and automated as well. This would be done in a similar way to setting up the SCIM integration, by running the SCIM creation command, which will generate a new token:

```
CREATE OR REPLACE SECURITY INTEGRATION <provisioner name>
    TYPE = scim
    SCIM_CLIENT = <SCIM client type>
    RUN_AS_ROLE = <provisioner role>;
```

Once that is done, you should retrieve the token again and update that in your IdP:

```
SELECT system$generate_scim_access_token('<provisioner name>');
```

SCIM access token does not support dual keys for a seamless rotation (like the one supported in user key-pair authentication), so you should either automate the process so that it happens when there is no provisioning, or expect the possibility of some failed API calls, and preferably run this process during a scheduled maintenance window.

Debugging and Monitoring SCIM

No matter which SCIM integration you're using, things can always go wrong (you made a copy-and-paste error with the token, there are network connection errors, etc.). There are two main places to look for when debugging. One is the logging done by your identity management platform, and the other is Snowflake. In Snowflake, the logs can be retrieved by the following SQL statements:

```
USE ROLE accountadmin;
USE <any database>.information_schema;
SELECT * FROM TABLE(rest_event_history('scim'));
```

You might want to run some more detailed query, such as the following, with the second parameter defining the "from timestamp" and the third defining the "to timestamp":

```
SELECT * FROM TABLE(
  rest_event_history('scim',
  DATEADD('hour', -2, CURRENT_TIMESTAMP()),
  CURRENT_TIMESTAMP()
);
```

This can be used for debugging, but can also be used for auditing and monitoring of your Snowflake data cloud. For more information about that, read Chapter 7, "Auditing and Monitoring."

4.2.2. User Provisioning Using SQL Integration

A different approach than using SCIM is to take leverage of the available SQL commands in Snowflake to manage users and create a provisioning layer that uses the underlying SQL commands to manage users and roles. The bottom line is that both methods can allow you to perform the actions of creating, modifying, and deleting users and roles, as well as assigning users to roles.

One advantage of provisioning using SQL integration is that if you intend to add more capabilities which are not supported by SCIM, you will be able to do so, assuming that you have the resources to spend in building such capabilities. One example is that you may choose to take advantage of role hierarchy in a way that's specific to your organization. You may also want to allocate resources like warehouses, masking or row access policies, or other assigning technical roles.

Provisioning using SQL integration takes advantage of the SQL commands for creating, modifying, and removing users and roles, and granting or revoking roles to users. For example, this SQL command will create a new user (TEST1), create a new role (MARKETINGOPS), and assign the user test1 to the MARKETINGOPS role:

```
CREATE USER TEST1;
CREATE ROLE MARKETINGOPS;
GRANT ROLE MARKETINGOPS TO USER TEST1;
```

This new role still does not have any privileges assigned to it (it can't actually access any data), and we will expand on that in Chapter 6, "Authorization: Data Access Control."

4.2.3. Combining SCIM and SQL Integration

This goes without saying, but we thought it would be good to mention that you can use both SCIM and SQL provisioning in parallel. A good example would be to provision your human users from your identity management system, while provisioning applications data access from a custom SQL provisioning. Another example would be to set the high-level access via SCIM integration, while building a self-service provisioning for temporary data access. More on that in Chapter 6, "Authorization: Data Access Control."

4.3. Authentication Types

After configuring the way users and roles are maintained in your Snowflake account, it is time to decide how users will be authenticated or, in other words, how will users "prove" their identity to Snowflake. As with most other Snowflake configurations, there is no "right answer" as to which authentication option to choose, but this is based on your usage of the system, organization structure, and other requirements. Regardless, we will try to point at the recommended way to configure authentication, per use case, to reduce risks.

There is a distinction in authentication between a "built-in" authentication method and a federated authentication. In the first, the service provider gets the credentials from the user and verifies them and thus verifies the identity of the user. In the latter, the credentials are verified by an identity provider. The authentication by a single service (the IdP), rather than by the different service providers, is called a Single Sign-On (SSO). Snowflake supports both methods, as described in the following.

4.3.1. Built-In Authentication

Snowflake's basic authentication is very easy to configure and use, and that's the built-in authentication. This basic authentication means assigning a password to each user, enabling users to specify the password using Snowflake's UI, (SnowSQL) command-line interface, or any other tool or application.

It is not only the easiest to configure. It is also, unfortunately, the least desired one in terms of security. Snowflake does not enforce password length or strength, and there is no option to automatically set password expiration. We advise you not to use user/password authentication, but rather use the more secure methods of authentication – SSO integration for human users and key-pair authentication for applications.

Having said that, if there are cases where you must use user/password authentication, we advise to make sure the risk is mitigated by placing additional controls. One is enabling the built-in multifactor authentication (MFA), as described later. Another is making sure that such users are not given access to sensitive data (which is often not the case – in many cases, it is accounts of high-privileged users). And yet another one is limiting access of such users to specific networks, so they will only be allowed to connect from certain IP ranges (e.g., corporate VPN, VPC, or office IP ranges).

Regardless of the type of authentication, and whether the user authentication is a human or an application, any authentication to your Snowflake account will be associated with a specific Snowflake user (even if the user is authenticated via federated access, the user will map to a Snowflake user, as discussed previously in the "User Provisioning" section).

To create a user, use the ***CREATE USER*** command. For example, to add the user Ben, with the password "averylongandcomplexpassword93920#@!", run the following SQL command:

```
CREATE USER BEN PASSWORD='averylongandcomplexpassword93920#@!';
```

Password Policy Enforcement

If you recall, we earlier gave an example where you can set a user's password to be a very short and weak password, such as "abc". This is due to Snowflake not validating the password's strength when you initially create a user. However, once the user is created, Snowflake enforces strong passwords. That means that passwords must be at least eight characters long, with at least one digit and at least one uppercase letter and one lowercase letter. As with any other password, do not reuse the same password you're using in another platform, and use a hard-to-guess password.

However, and this is a crucial point often overlooked by administrators, the password policy **only applies after the user's first login**. This means that if an admin sets a new user account by running

`CREATE USER` TEST1 PASSWORD=`'abc'`;

the user will be able to log in with the password abc. Furthermore, unless the user logged in, the password can also be altered by

`ALTER USER` TEST1 SET PASSWORD=`'abc'`;

Only after a user's first login would the password be forced to be a strong one. The reasoning is that an admin can set a user with an easy password for their first login, so that the user would change it to a strong one later. We believe that this is not a good practice and recommend the following:

- Once again, use SSO for user logins over the built-in password management. This will enforce all your organization's policies and will not require having "yet another credential."

- Even if you're setting an initial password, make it a strong one. There's no reason, even for an initial password, to use a weak password. The reason is that even in the short while between creating a user and gaining ownership over one, that user can be compromised. In addition, when other users know that initial passwords are weak, this even increases the risks of an attempted account takeover due to password guessing.

- Whenever you're setting a new user, set the MUST_CHANGE_
  PASSSWORD parameter to true, as in the following example:

```
CREATE USER BEN
PASSWORD='The l0ng & wind1ng p@ssw0o0rd!',
MUST_CHANGE_PASSWORD=TRUE;
```

Client Sessions Keep Alive

An important parameter is the CLIENT_SESSION_KEEP_ALIVE parameter. This parameter defines whether the users' sessions are kept alive when the user is idle or whether they're terminated after four hours, forcing the user to log in again. This parameter can be set in the account, user, or specific session scope and should be kept to false (which means the session should renew).

Multifactor Authentication (MFA) in Snowflake

Authenticating a user using only a username and password is a problem. Many users reuse passwords or choose an easy-to-guess password or their passwords leak for other reasons, and you don't want a stranger inside your data cloud, right? If you don't have an integration with a SSO provider, Snowflake also offers out-of-the-box multifactor authentication. This means that users will not only be authenticated by "something they know" (their password), but also with "something they have" (a token that they will get from the two-factor authentication provider, Duo Mobile).

The MFA support in Snowflake is both for connections to the web UI and for connections done using the SnowSQL command-line interface or other clients connected with JDBC/ODBC.

Snowflake MFA also supports caching of the MFA token, meaning that you will not need to enter the token every time you log in, rather it will be stored locally for a certain period of time (up to four hours). In many organizations, this would be in-line with the security guidelines, but not in all of them. Consult with your security team, and in case you want to set it off (e.g., if MFA is only used for fallback authentication in extreme edge cases by admins), you can turn it off using the ALLOW_CLIENT_MFA_CACHING account-level parameter.

Setting Up MFA in Snowflake

MFA in Snowflake is available to all account levels and is done in a self-service manner, meaning that the users enroll themselves to MFA. This is done from the web UI, by going to *Preferences* (in the upper right corner of the web interface). There, under *Multi-factor Authentication*, you will find the enrollment link, as in Figure 4-9.

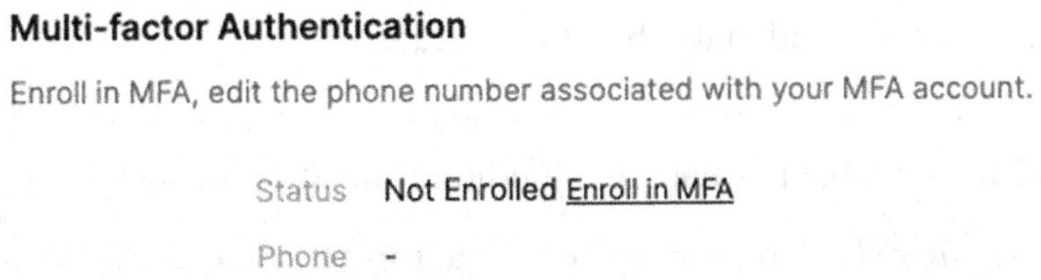

Multi-factor Authentication

Enroll in MFA, edit the phone number associated with your MFA account.

Status   **Not Enrolled** Enroll in MFA

Phone   -

Figure 4-9. Multi-factor Authentication enrollment

This will take you through an enrollment process, including installation of the Duo Mobile application and setting up using a QR code to be scanned. Unfortunately, only this specific authentication application is used, and if you're already using another MFA application (such as Google Authenticator which is a very common and free option), you'll need to have "yet another app" on your mobile.

As an account administrator, from time to time, you may need to disable users' MFA temporarily or to reset completely. To disable MFA temporarily for a user, you use the *ALTER USER* command, with the *MINS_TO_BYPASS_MFA* parameter. For example, to allow Jason to log in without MFA for an hour, you would run the following SQL command:

```
ALTER USER JASON SET MINS_TO_BYPASS_MFA=60;
```

You can view that parameter by running

```
DESCRIBE USER JASON;
```

To completely reset the MFA token for Jason, you will need to run the following:

```
ALTER USER test1 SET DISABLE_MFA=TRUE;
```

Once you've done that, you need to instruct Jason to enroll again from Snowflake's web UI.

So... Should You Use It?

You will probably not want to use this for your entire user base. While multifactor authentication is important, it is best to be used with your organization's SSO provider. Using the built-in MFA capability is less desirable in our view from the following reasons:

- With this feature, we need to ask our users to enroll through the web UI, install yet another application (which in many organizations is frowned upon), and make their lives harder.

- We need to create a process around following that users actually do that (more on that in Chapter 7, "Auditing and Monitoring").

In most cases, there is no reason to use the built-in MFA. We would recommend reserving that for the following cases:

- A small organization without an SSO provider or until SSO is set up.

- For risk mitigation purposes. For example, when you want to set up a Snowflake user in addition to the SSO users, in case of SSO failure.

- For added security in specific cases, for example, only for admin users.

4.3.2. Federation: Single Sign-On (SSO) Integration

In most cases, this would be the recommended authentication method for human users to your organization's Snowflake account. Using a federated environment means that your users will not authenticate directly with Snowflake (the service provider), but with your organization's identity provider (IdP), which will be trusted by Snowflake to authenticate users.

SAML 2.0 and SSO

In federated authentication, there are two types of services: the identity provider (IdP) and the service provider (SP). In our case, the SP is Snowflake, and the IdP is your organization's IdP. They communicate over a protocol called SAML 2.0.

SAML (stands for Security Assertion Markup Language) is an open standard for exchanging authentication and authorization data between IdPs and SPs, based on XML messages passed. In a federated authentication, the user authenticates against the IdP, and the SP then asserts the authentication.

Note that SAML SSO authentication can either be initiated by the SP (Snowflake) or by the IdP (as a link in the IdP or a dashboard with buttons for all of your authorized applications). When the authentication is initiated by the IdP, the user is authenticated and then redirected to the SP. When the authentication is initiated by the SP, the user is redirected from the SP to the IdP for authentication and then redirected back to the SP.

To read more about SAML 2.0, visit `http://docs.oasis-open.org/security/saml/Post2.0/sstc-saml-tech-overview-2.0.html`, or for even more in-depth discussion of SAML, OAuth, and more, refer to *Solving Identity Management in Modern Applications: Demystifying OAuth 2.0, OpenID Connect, and SAML 2.0* by Yvonne Wilson and Abhishek Hingnikar (Apress, 2019).

The advantages were already mentioned, but let's go over them again:

- Users will not need to have one more password to remember, also exposing more risks as users tend to reuse passwords, not use strong enough passwords, or leak their passwords in other ways (e.g., by a phishing campaign).

- Having strong password policies, password change policies, and multifactor authentication built in and working reduces security risks.

- This is also easier for compliance, as, assuming the SSO processes are well defined, meeting the same with Snowflake makes it more simple to meet compliance requirements.

- You, as a Snowflake administrator, will not need to babysit your users (resetting their MFA tokens, setting initial passwords, etc.), as well as monitor all of this to reduce risk. You will then have more time on your hands and can use it to read this book.

Federated authentication enables the following processes:

- Most importantly, it enables Snowflake login using SSO.

- Logging out.

- Session timeout.

Once you have configured (as per the following) the SSO flow, users will be able to log in directly from the identity provider (from their applications "desktop" or "dashboard"). It is optional, yet recommended, to also allow users to initiate the authentication from Snowflake, as described in the following, by setting the account parameter sso_login_page to true. This will add a button redirecting to the SSO authentication from Snowflake's login screen.

An important thing to note is that simply setting up federation does not cancel "regular" logins, and if a user goes to your organization's Snowflake login page or uses a valid login and password combination in any tool or application, they will still be authenticated. Therefore, if you are migrating your users from being local Snowflake users to being federated using an IdP, we remind you that you also need to disable their ability to log in locally by altering the user's password to be blank. For example, to disable Jason's login credentials from working directly with Snowflake, run the following command:

```
ALTER USER JASON SET PASSWORD='';
```

It is also important to note that logging out of an identity provider, in most cases, will not force your Snowflake user outside of an existing Snowflake session, but will only trigger the need for a federated login in the next time they either experience a session timeout or log in again to Snowflake.

Setting Up SAML 2.0 Federated Authentication

As with other integrations (discussed in the SCIM section), Snowflake supports usage of SAML 2.0, but with certain identity providers, there is an easier built-in integration. At the time of writing, there is a native support in both Okta and Microsoft ADFS. You can set SSO working in other providers as well, though it would require a bit more customization work.

Setting Up SSO Integration with Okta

We'll start by setting up SAML 2.0 integration with Okta, to allow a Single Sign-On (SSO) connection if your organization uses Okta as its IdP. If you still haven't integrated Snowflake with Okta, you may refer to the beginning of this chapter, where we introduce the basics, including how to set up a free trial Okta account, in case you don't have one and would still like to experiment. The directions here assume that you already have an Okta account and that you've set up the initial Snowflake application.

Go to your Okta account, and enter the admin section. Once inside, hit the **Applications** tab, and choose the Snowflake application (if it is not set up yet, set it up, as per the instructions in the beginning of this chapter). Now choose **Sign On** in the navigation bar, and click the button **View Setup Instructions**, which will open a new browser window with the certificate and SSO URL to configure in Snowflake. The certificate is used so that Snowflake can trust the SAML messages coming from Okta, and the SSO URL is used to redirect users who are not yet authenticated to Okta for authentication. After that, go to the original Okta configuration screen and hit Save.

Note that in Snowflake's login dialog screen, in addition to the SSO login button, the user will also be able to authenticate using a username and password. If you want to disable that, you will need to unset the user's password or set it to an empty string.

To configure that in Snowflake, head into your Snowflake web UI (note: you can run the SQL commands from other clients as well, but we found the web UI the most comfortable for such configurations), and make sure you're using a sufficient role. Now write the following SQL command in the worksheet:

```
ALTER ACCOUNT SET saml_identity_provider = '{
  "certificate": "<YOUR CERTIFICATE>",
  "ssoUrl": "<YOUR SSO URL>",
  "type": "OKTA"
}';
```

In addition, to activate the SP initiated SSO login link, run the following SQL command:

```
ALTER ACCOUNT SET sso_login_page = true;
```

Note that when logging in, your Okta users must be configured in your Snowflake as well. This can be done manually or of course in a much more provisioned way by provisioning the users as described previously in the "SCIM Integration" section.

Setting Up SSO Integration with Other SAML 2.0 Providers

As previously mentioned, Okta is not the only identity provider supported by Snowflake, but having a preset Snowflake application helps make configuration and integration easier. Another option is to configure SAML to work with Microsoft ADFS. The configuration on the Snowflake end is pretty much the same, except that the type of SAML IdP should be ADFS, as the following:

```
ALTER ACCOUNT SET saml_identity_provider = '{
  "certificate": "<YOUR CERTIFICATE>",
  "ssoUrl": "<YOUR SSO URL>",
  "type": "ADFS"
}';
```

Note that the certificate has to be without new lines, which is either done in a text editor as a manual process or by script as part of an automated process.

The configuration and certificate issuing in Microsoft ADFS are a bit more complicated than Okta, and you can follow the documentation at the following page to do so:

```
https://docs.snowflake.com/en/user-guide/admin-security-fed-auth-configure-
idp.html#ad-fs-setup
```

In the same way, you can set custom SAML 2.0 integration with other identity providers. For example, in **Ping Identity**, you will need to configure a new SAML application in the following path in your administrator console: **Applications ➤ Add Application ➤ Web App ➤ SAML**.

In each identity provider, you will need to follow the documentation of setting a custom SAML application, by using your account's federated authentication login (https://<YOUR ACCOUNT>.snowflakecomputing.com/fed/login) and federated logout URL (https://<YOUR ACCOUNT>.snowflakecomputing.com/fed/logout). Once configured, you will get the certificate and SSO URL from the SAML metadata, so that you can configure Snowflake to trust your IdP.

The bad news is that each identity provider is slightly different, and configuring the integration may require some translation between terms in different applications. The good news is that you will probably only need to configure the integration in a single identity provider that your organization uses (they don't call it Single Sign On for nothing), and you or the people in charge of this platform (in most cases, it's IT) already have an experience in integrating other applications.

SSO for Code

We draw a line between any production-ready code (where it is well tested, audited, and secrets are retrieved using a proper deployment process) and any other code being run by engineers, analysts, data scientists, and others. The latter are not truly an application accessing data, but a human accessing data, and for the same reasons you want humans to have SSO (leading to a security policy including MFA) when they're connected by the web UI or other tools to Snowflake, you want the same level of security when they connect directly.

Fortunately, though it's more simple to connect without it, it does not complicate things a lot, and we recommend to apply SSO for humans running scripts, unless there is a very good reason to do otherwise (i.e., tests with a test account and no live data).

Python is very popular for ad hoc scripting and has very rich support for machine learning libraries and is thus often used by data consumers to analyze data, transform it, and make other use of it. To connect with Python using SSO, instead of using a username/password connection, use the authenticator option:

```
ctx = snowflake.connector.connect(
    account='<YOUR ACCOUNT>',
    host='<YOUR ACCOUNT>.snowflakecomputing.com',
    authenticator='externalbrowser',
    warehouse='compute_wh',
    user='<CONNECTING USER>'
    )
```

When you run a script with this connection, the application will show the following message:

Initiating login request with your identity provider. A browser window should have opened for you to complete the login. If you can't see it, check existing browser windows, or your OS settings. Press CTRL+C to abort and try again...

As per the message, it will also open a browser window to authenticate your connection using your identity provider.

Another popular method used for ad hoc command-line queries is SnowSQL, in which you can do the same by adding the following command-line parameter: *--authenticator externalbrowser*.

The *authenticator=externalbrowser* parameter can be also used in JDBC and .NET connection parameters, and in ODBC, you can set this parameter by editing odbc.ini (Linux) or by using regedit in Windows.

SSO Connection Caching

It is recommended to use SSO connection caching in cases where there is heavy usage of SSO for code, as otherwise users will need to go through the federated authentication each time they run their scripts. This means that the application will store the connection token in the key store of the operating system and will use that for a certain amount of time instead of requesting a login each time.

To allow that, run the following command as an administrator:

```
ALTER ACCOUNT SET allow_id_token = true;
```

Note that not all clients support this (at the time of writing, only the Python, JDBC, and ODBC connectors), and some may need additional packages to be installed. For Python, you would need to install the following extra of the snowflake connector: "snowflake-connector-python[secure-local-storage]".

SSO with Automated Okta Authentication

Currently, only available in the Okta integration, you can configure SSO to work without opening an external browser window. However, it will require passing the SSO credentials in the connection string (you will not be prompted to insert them, you must provide them). This can backfire if it causes users to put their SSO credentials inside their scripts, so we advise to use this cautiously. To do that, you use the following parameter:

```
authenticator='https://<YOUR OKTA ACCOUNT>.okta.com'
```

SSO for BI Tools

A common use case for humans connecting to Snowflake is by using BI Tools, and often this is done by providing a specific Snowflake user for that BI tool. We recommend against that, as you want each user to be identified separately from a security and governance point of view. Instead, you should use OAuth integration when possible, in which the authentication is performed by Snowflake (or by integration through an identity provider), and your BI tool gets a temporary token to use for querying.

OAuth integration for BI tools is available, as the time of writing, in Tableau and Looker, and is set up with the following SQL command, which you run as an ACCOUNTADMIN:

```
CREATE OR REPLACE SECURITY INTEGRATION tableau
TYPE = OAUTH
ENABLED = TRUE
OAUTH_CLIENT = tableau_server
OAUTH_ISSUE_REFRESH_TOKENS = TRUE
OAUTH_REFRESH_TOKEN_VALIDITY = <SECONDS>
BLOCKED_ROLES_LIST = ('ACCOUNTADMIN', 'SYSADMIN', 'DATA_UPDATER');
```

This example configures OAuth for Tableau Server, but you can also adjust it to support the rest of the BI tools. Some important security considerations are the amount of seconds after which an access token is invalidated and the user needs to re-authenticate and, most importantly, a list of roles which will be restricted from being used by this OAuth integration. We will discuss more about roles and data access in Chapter 6, "Authorization: Data Access Control."

Another thing to note is that OAuth authentication will also lead to users being individually authenticated, instead of having one "service account" for all the data access done from the BI tools. Although some may see this as a pollution of your logs and users listing, this gives a much more granular reporting of the actual users who were accessing the data.

4.3.3. Nonhuman Authentication

Not only humans, scripts, and tools connect to Snowflake. In many cases, you'd want to connect Snowflake to applications without human interaction for different reasons. In such cases, we advise against using a simple approach of a user and password authentication, though in some cases it is impossible to circumvent (i.e., due to usage of legacy code, or if your application does not support key-pair authentication, such as Node.js or .NET applications).

The cases where only a user and password are used by an application are a soft spot, and the risks imposed by this should be mitigated. Though the exact steps depend on the details, we recommend to take the following precautions:

- Make sure that the user being used by the application has very strict privileges, allowing it to do exactly what it needs to do. If it needs to update the "candy costs" table, give it update privilege to the candy costs table and no more.

- Make sure that you set a dedicated user for the application and not reuse the user for usage in other applications or – even worse – used by humans as well.

- Use a different user for development, staging, and production.

- Make sure that you're using hard-to-guess passwords.

- Compensate with network policies (see Chapter 5, "Network Access Control").

- Monitor well, as per Chapter 7, "Auditing and Monitoring."

Key-Pair Authentication

Whenever possible, though, a stronger authentication is recommended, which is a key-pair authentication. In this method of authentication, you generate a private and public key pair and configure the public key in Snowflake, and only a user connecting with the private certificate is able to connect to Snowflake.

Support is pretty wide, including SnowSQL, Python, Spark and Kafka connectors, Go Driver, JDBC, and ODBC. It is noted, however, that at the time of writing, it is not supported in .NET and Node.js.

To set up key-pair authentication, you will need to first generate the certificate and then configure the public key in Snowflake. First, let's generate the certificate. This can either be an encrypted or unencrypted key, where we recommend using an encrypted key, though this would depend on the scenario and is not needed in all cases (consult with your security team about the specific case). Generating the certificate can be done from command-line using openssl.

First, from a terminal window on your machine (and afterward as part of your deployment process), generate the private key, and choose a password for encrypting it:

```
openssl genrsa 2048 | opopenssl genrsa 2048 | openssl pkcs8 -topk8 -inform
PEM -out rsa_key.p8
```

If you don't want to password encrypt it, add the -nocrypt flag to the command. Next, generate the public key:

```
openssl genrsa 2048 | opopenssl rsa -in rsa_key.p8 -pubout -out rsa_key.pub
```

Now, edit your public key file (rsa_key.pub), and eliminate line breaks from the certificate, and run the following SQL command as a Snowflake administrator:

```
ALTER USER <YOUR USER> SET rsa_public_key='<YOUR KEY>';
```

Once this is configured, you're good to go. You have the private key, and Snowflake has the means to authenticate it (by using the public key). You can use the following Python script to test the connection:

```python
import snowflake.connector
import os
from cryptography.hazmat.backends import default_backend
from cryptography.hazmat.primitives.asymmetric import rsa
from cryptography.hazmat.primitives.asymmetric import dsa
from cryptography.hazmat.primitives import serialization

# for testing:
os.environ['PRIVATE_KEY_PASSPHRASE'] = '<YOUR PASSWORD>'

with open("./rsa_key.p8", "rb") as key:
    p_key= serialization.load_pem_private_key(
        key.read(),
        password=os.environ['PRIVATE_KEY_PASSPHRASE'].encode(),
        backend=default_backend()
    )

pkb = p_key.private_bytes(
    encoding=serialization.Encoding.DER,
    format=serialization.PrivateFormat.PKCS8,
    encryption_algorithm=serialization.NoEncryption())
```

```
ctx = snowflake.connector.connect(
    user='<YOUR USER>',
    account='<YOUR ACCOUNT>',
    host='<YOUR ACCOUNT>.snowflakecomputing.com',
    private_key=pkb,
    warehouse='<YOUR WAREHOUSE>',
    database='<YOUR DB>',
    schema='<YOUR SCHEMA>'
    )

cs = ctx.cursor()
```

Using Key-Pair Authentication in Production

There is a common misconception, in which things like key-pair encryption are magical creatures which automagically protects everything and once implemented makes everything using them or surrounding them completely secure. It is important to remind you that when you connect using the private key, you are using a very secure channel to connect to your Snowflake. However, if anyone else is using the private key, they enjoy the same connection to your Snowflake account.

In other words, it is imperative that you keep your secrets secret. In the last section, we created a local key pair, which is great for development and testing purposes, but in production (as well as in staging), it is important to make key creation automated as part of the deployment, or at least handled correctly, without leaving local copies of private keys, instead using vaults to pull them and inject them into containers or otherwise use them securely in your applications.

The public key still has to be configured in Snowflake, but is obviously less sensitive than the private key and can either be updated manually or automatically. We recommend automating the rotation of key pairs by writing specific deployment scripts as per the following section, as part of a healthy DataSecOps operation.

Rotating Your Key Pairs

It is important to rotate your keys based on your security procedures. This limits the risk of a leaked key to a certain period in time. Fortunately, Snowflake enables a "hotswap" possibility to make a key-pair rotation without downtime or errors during the rotation period. To rotate your keys, generate a new public-private pair (as per the previous section), and then run the following:

```
ALTER USER <YOUR USER> SET rsa_public_key_2='<YOUR KEY>';
```

Now, once you deploy your applications with the new private key, you will unset the old key by using the following command:

```
ALTER USER <YOUR USER> UNSET rsa_public_key;
```

The next time you are changing the key pair, you will do the opposite (configure the key in rsa_public_key, and then once you deploy the new private key, unset rsa_public_key_2).

Snowflake SQL API

Snowflake has a preview feature (at the time of writing), which allows users to send queries to Snowflake using a REST API, instead of through connectors or the web UI. This API currently only supports sending single queries in a synchronous or asynchronous way, but this will probably expand over time.

You can either authenticate using an OAuth token you retrieve or by a key-pair authentication. For more information about OAuth authentication, refer to Section 4.3.2.3, and for more information about public-private keys, refer to Section 4.3.3.1. The specific way in which you authenticate using these secrets is specified in the documentation here (`https://docs.snowflake.com/en/developer-guide/sql-api/guide.html#authenticating-to-the-server`).

SQL API Security Notes

The following are some security notes to be aware of when using the SQL REST API:

- If the SQL API is used to send user-generated content, make sure the input is validated or properly escaped prior to running the queries. This can be done by parameter binding, per Section 4.3.3.3.

- If used in production, make sure that the secrets (private keys and OAuth tokens) are generated automatically and placed in vaults, per your security handling of secrets.

- Make sure you only use a user with the role required for the action performed by the API, and not an overprivileged role.

Preventing SQL Injection in Application Queries

If the applications receive input from users, make sure you pass the input using data binding, instead of by concatenating them to a SQL command. This is done to prevent SQL injection attacks. As an example, if regional sales people of ACME Candies has an internal portal, through which they can retrieve data about their deals, and it receives the city as a variable, if a "normal" query for deals in NYC looks like this:

```
SELECT deal_name, deal_size FROM deals WHERE city = 'NYC';
```

A curious user who wants to retrieve all data may put *nyc' OR 1 --* as an input, which will now list all results instead (the OR 1 adds a boolean expression that is always true, and the -- comments out the rest of the query to prevent additional filtering), resulting in the following query being executed:

```
SELECT deal_name, deal_size FROM deals WHERE city = 'NYC' OR 1 -- '
```

An even more curious user may also retrieve data from other tables, using UNION, for example, by sending *xxx' UNION ALL SELECT name, phone FROM sensitive_table --* as value:

```
SELECT deal_name, deal_size FROM deals WHERE city = 'xxx' UNION ALL SELECT name, phone FROM sensitive_table --
```

These risks should also be handled when authorizing data, and you will learn more about that, including giving access only to specific rows of data within a Snowflake table, in Chapter 6, "Authorization: Data Access Control."

An example of using parameter binding in Snowflake (Python):

```
con.cursor().execute(
    "SELECT id, name FROM models WHERE type = %s", ("type", )
    )
```

4.3.4. Compensating Factors in Authentication

During this chapter, we discussed ideal authentication for your human and nonhuman Snowflake users. Life is not always ideal, and sometimes, you will be challenged by requirements that will prevent you from immediately applying the optimal authentication methods.

A good example to that is BI tools that do not support OAuth authentication. If your organization is using such tools, it will probably not replace such BI tools overnight, and so you will want to establish compensating factors around that usage. These compensating factors can be both by strengthening the authentication (e.g., by adding network policies) and by limiting the impact of the users using such BI tools by giving them only the privileges they need for the BI tool usage (the role granted can have only select access and be further limited by row and column access policies, per Chapter 6, "Authorization: Data Access Control").

When dealing with compensating factors, remember that your main goal is to enable data access while reducing risk. Depending on the structure of your organization, you may want (or need) to consult with the security or GRC teams around some of these risks and the alternative solutions.

4.4. Summary

In this chapter, we've discussed the ways in which you provision users in your Snowflake data cloud, as well as how you authenticate users, whether they're humans or applications, and discussed the security implications and recommendations in each case. We did cover a lot of ground and important ground as well. We know that your situation is not necessarily perfect at the moment, but now is a good time to note to yourself the main gaps you see, if you have an active organization running Snowflake, and start reducing some of the risks before proceeding to the next chapters (or you can do that in parallel).

In addition, we discussed some compensating factors which you should consider, and we urge you to use them not only when "all else fails," and you're using a less recommended form of authentication, but in any case you can, to reduce risks.

For your convenience, we're also adding the following simplified flow to help you make authentication decisions in Snowflake:

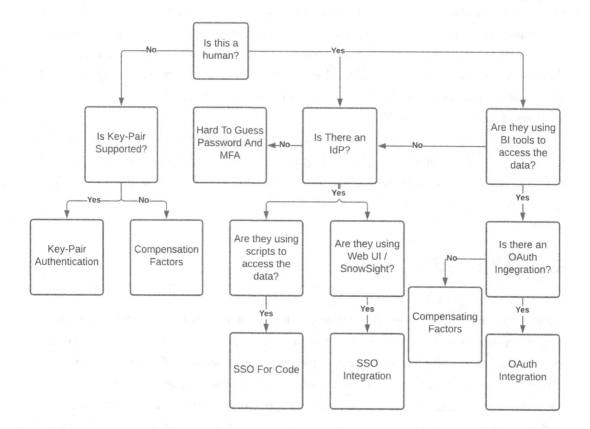

CHAPTER 5

Network Access Control

Network access control is quite a blunt tool, which is not necessarily a bad thing. What this means is that you want to place access controls to your data warehouse based on the network origin of the traffic. This can be a quick and effective way to reduce security risks, as well as sometimes being part of compliance requirements (to have, as well as show that you have network access policies placed on top of your data access).

When it comes to reducing security risks, this is quite simple. For example, if we have an application user, to be used by a production application, there is no reason for it to communicate with our data warehouse from anything other than a specific set of IP addresses. In the same way, we may want all the traffic to our account to come only from specific sets of IP addresses, such as our office IPs, VPNs, and VPCs.

Although network blocking is not a bulletproof method to prevent all risks, it is quite effective to lower the attack surface of potential attackers, as well as to restrict users from putting your organization at risk because they are careless and wanted to run "just one query" from an insecure home network.

In addition to network access policies, which handles traffic done over the public Internet, Snowflake also offers direct traffic from your VPC using PrivateLinks, which we will also discuss.

5.1. How Do Network Access Policies Work?

In Snowflake, you create objects called network policies. These objects consist of a list of IP ranges to allow access from, and optionally, a list of IP ranges to disallow access from. The disallowed IP ranges are within the allowed IP ranges (as anything outside of the allowed ranges is disallowed by default).

67

© Ben Herzberg, Yoav Cohen 2022
B. Herzberg and Y. Cohen, *Snowflake Security*, https://doi.org/10.1007/978-1-4842-7389-0_5

This is a sample network policy creation, which allows access from any IP in the IP range, inserted within the CIDR format, of 6.6.6.0 to 6.6.6.255, excluding 6.6.6.1:

```
CREATE NETWORK POLICY candy_office
ALLOWED_IP_LIST = ('6.6.6.6/24')
BLOCKED_IP_LIST = ('6.6.6.1/32');
```

Those policies can be then used as a parameter in either your entire account, which will be active for any user attempting to connect, or for specific users. If there is an account-wide network policy, and a certain user also has a user network policy set, the specific user network policy will determine whether the user will be able to connect. In addition to the regular account and user scope, network policies can also be set on security integrations, as we've seen in the previous chapter.

5.1.1. Setting Up Account-Level Network Policy

Once you have a network policy set up, as explained previously, to set it up on the account, you need to assign the policy to the account, using the following command:

```
ALTER ACCOUNT SET NETWORK_POLICY="candy_office";
```

Note that if the network policy does not enable the current IP you're sending the query from, you will not be able to assign it (as you don't want to get locked out of your own network).

5.1.2. Setting Up User-Level Network Policy

Setting up a user's network policy is also pretty straightforward and is done with the following command:

```
ALTER USER BEN_SWEETTOOTH SET NETWORK_POLICY='CANDY_OFFICE';
```

Note that the network policy in an "alter user" has to be upper case.

To cancel either an account- or user-level network policy assignment, you can use the UNSET command, for example:

```
ALTER USER BEN_SWEETTOOTH UNSET NETWORK_POLICY;
```

5.1.3. Limitations

There are several limitations in Snowflake's network policies model. Let's mention them, as well as some options to work around them.

No Group-Level Granularity

Since there is no notion of groups in Snowflake, there is also no notion of groups of users with policies per group. Sure, there could have been one assigned per role, but that would have been confusing as well, in terms of conflicts between certain different roles that a user holds. This limitation means that you can either set a policy for the entire account or for a specific user, but you have no option in between.

One obvious option is to use what you have, in which case you actually set a policy for your entire account, and if there are exclusions, you set them on a personal basis. However, this does not scale gracefully. When you have dozens of users or more, and you want to apply network policies in an effective way, it gets difficult to scale, and you either spend too much time setting up and assigning policies or you cut corners, and either give slow service to your data consumers or make sacrifices about your security risk level.

Workarounds

One possible solution is to run a recurring cron job, which will run periodically, and set network policies according to specific characteristics, such as if they have specific roles which propagated to the user account from the IdP, or in another way. For example, if in ACME Candies there is a network policy specific to offices, a script can retrieve the list of users with that role, then execute the ALTER USER commands.

Such a query can be:

```
SELECT CONCAT('ALTER USER ', grantee_name, ' SET NETWORK_POLICY=\
'SFO_OFFICE\';') AS cmd
FROM snowflake.account_usage.grants_to_users
WHERE DELETED_ON IS NULL
AND ROLE = 'SFO_OFFICE';
```

Another way, at least for IdP provisioned users, is to set network restrictions in the IdP, so that authentication will not be possible, according to a specific network policy. In other words, users will not be able to log in to your Snowflake account because of external network policies.

No Granularity Within Account

Another limitation in the network policies is that the network policies are for all access to the account, and can't be granular within the account itself. As an example, if ACME Candies has several databases in their Snowflake account, and they want access to the HR database to only be done from the office, this can't be done with Snowflake network policies.

Workarounds

One possibility is, of course, to separate such databases to a separate account and have one account that's only accessible from certain networks. This may be easier said than done if we're not designing a new account, but need to change architecture on a moving target. This may need to include changes to data pipelines, authentication changes in the new account, setting up user provisioning, and changing connections and applications. In other words, it's a lot easier when planning ahead.

Network Policies Are Only IPv4

Another limitation is that the network policies (at the time of writing) don't support IPv6 network ranges, but only IPv4. This currently has no workaround, and if that's the case, you can try Snowflake's support, in case they can work out something specific for your account.

5.2. PrivateLink Integrations

Network policies are great for most of the use cases. Snowflake is a cloud data service, and as such, it makes sense that access to it is done over the Internet. However, in certain cases, such as highly regulated industries, you want to completely eliminate traffic being transferred over the public Internet, even though (as we've learned in Chapter 3, "Data Encryption and Ingestion") data in transit is always sent encrypted.

The reasons for using PrivateLink are mainly either that the organization is required to do so due to compliance requirements (either directly or through interpretation of a risk assessment) or in case of a security requirement. Keep in mind that in addition to having to set up a PrivateLink, it also comes as part of the business critical plan, so it may incur additional costs. As it integrates with your public cloud's private link, it may incur costs in your public cloud billing as well.

Setting up a new PrivateLink is done by first requesting Snowflake to start a PrivateLink integration, which would require sending the VPC you want to connect from (or more than one in case there's more than one). This is done manually, through support or in case needed through your account manager. Once this is done, follow the documentation to set up the PrivateLink, whether this is AWS PrivateLink or Azure PrivateLink.

An important point to consider is that once you finish configuring your PrivateLink, you also need to add an account-level network policy to allow access to your Snowflake account only from the VPC (for more information, see the earlier section about network policies).

5.3. Summary

Snowflake offers several options to control your data access based on your network origin. These include allowing and blocking access to your Snowflake account based on network policies, either to an entire account or to specific users, and the option to have traffic transferred within the public cloud's network (without going out to the Internet) for increased security. The latter option requires additional work in setting up, and incurs costs, and is mainly used in heavily regulated industries or where there is a significant security risk.

CHAPTER 6

Authorization: Data Access Control

In ACME Candies' offices, not everybody can go everywhere, even once you went through the receptionist. Only candy makers go into the kitchen, only finance teams can access the finance rooms, some of the rooms are only available during business hours, and so on. There's a good reason for that – if we let everybody go everywhere, we induce risk.

The same can be said about the data you store in Snowflake. In most cases, allowing everybody to have access to everything is not a good plan. As we discussed in the introduction to this book, wanting to make more use of more data by more people is probably one of the reasons you started using Snowflake in the first place. However, in addition to the value that users bring by analyzing data, users with access to the data also have its costs in terms of risk. The reason is that some of your data may have certain levels of sensitivity, and having access to it increases the risk of sensitive data leakage.

Another challenge when limiting access to data is the burden it places on Snowflake administrators (usually the data engineering teams), as they need to actually provide access to specific data within the data warehouse. The more granular your data access control is, the more potential overhead is added to these individuals, and as this may very well be you reading this book (fourth wall alert), it may be good to discuss strategies to lower that overhead.

It is important to note that providing data access is hard, and in many cases, what you do depends on current and future usage of the data by its consumers. That is why it is extremely important to make sure that data consumers are consulted with throughout the process, which may save a lot of time and aggravation when limitations are put in place.

© Ben Herzberg, Yoav Cohen 2022
B. Herzberg and Y. Cohen, *Snowflake Security*, https://doi.org/10.1007/978-1-4842-7389-0_6

In this chapter, we will discuss data access control methodologies in general, the Snowflake access control model, and different strategies around actually allowing data access to people in ways that take into account security, compliance, privacy, and operational overhead.

6.1. Data Access Models

Though we are sure that you are familiar with at least some data access models, we will give a short overview of the relevant access control models, to give a better context for when we deal with Snowflake's access control model. If you want to dive deep into access control models, you can find more references on this book's website (https://snowflake-security.com), or you can refer to the book ***Authentication and Access Control***.

6.1.1. MAC (Mandatory Access Control)

Mandatory access control is an access control model in which a centralized system controls access to objects, which is usually done based on labels (such as, based on its military origins, top secret, secret, or confidential), and certain security clearances for users. These labels are mostly coupled with a project clearance. If implemented at ACME, if ACME Candies' recipes are labeled ***top secret***, and an employee without a sufficient level of clearance tries to access them, they are not granted access to them. Also, if a certain employee has a top secret access level, but no access to the specific project, they will not have access to the recipes.

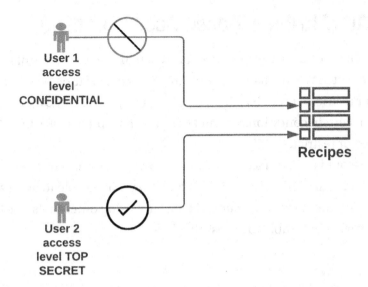

Since mandatory access control is system-wide, it is less suitable for data warehouses like Snowflake, where you want the ability for users to set access to objects and need a more robust way of access control.

6.1.2. DAC (Discretionary Access Control)

In contrast to mandatory access control, discretionary access control is allowing or limiting access to objects based on users and groups and the configuration settings for them. The main difference between the mandatory and discretionary access control models is that in a discretionary access control system, users can pass the permissions they own to other users (e.g., grant access). This makes the access control more decentralized than MAC.

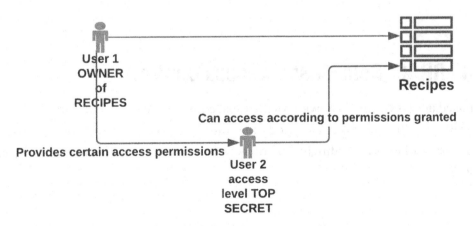

6.1.3. ABAC (Attribute-Based Access Control)

Also known as policy-based access control (PBAC). In this access control model, certain attributes are collected when a user attempts to access the secured object, and the system allows or restricts access based on a policy. The policies follow an "if … then" process, where if certain conditions are met (a boolean result of true), then based on that access is allowed or restricted.

An example would be that if a data scientist from ACME Candies attempts to access financial data, and they are using a BI tool, they will be able to access the data. However, if they attempt to access financial data, and using other tools (such as scripting languages), they will not be able to access the data.

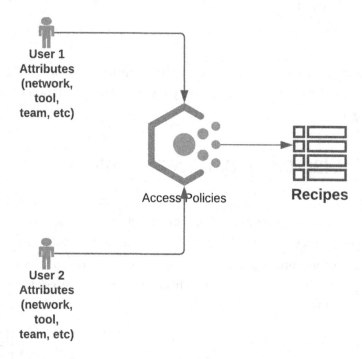

6.1.4. RBAC (Role-Based Access Control)

Role-based access control is nowadays the most common access control model in organizations, where users are assigned roles and the privileges are set per role, which gives access to objects accordingly. The roles define a set of permissions that are given to the users.

The "abstraction layer" added by giving roles to users and assigning the permissions to the roles, as opposed to directly giving permissions to the users, enables managing permissions in scale.

There is no conflict between RBAC and DAC or MAC, and as we will see (spoiler alert), Snowflake indeed has a combination of both RBAC and DAC.

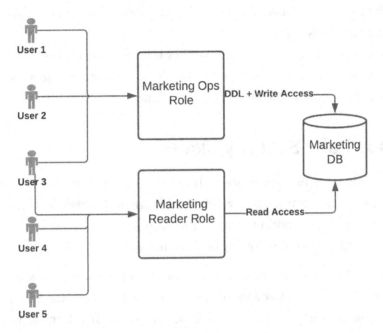

In this figure, users are assigned to roles. For example, user 1 and user 2 are assigned to the marketing operations role which allows DDL commands (data definition language) and write access on the marketing DB. User 4 and user 5 have read access, because they are granted the marketing reader role. User 3 is granted with both roles, so they can have both read and write permissions.

6.2. Snowflake Access Control Model

Snowflake's access control model combines elements of RBAC and DAC. In Snowflake (unlike many other databases like Postgres, MySQL, Oracle, and many others), you can't assign access privileges directly to users and can only assign them to roles, which are then assigned to users. In addition, in Snowflake, each object (also known as "securable object," as it's an object which you can secure access to) has an owner, who can grant access to the object.

This access model has a good intention, which is to better align Snowflake to the modern RBAC way of granting access, eliminating the mess that sometimes occurs when users are granted direct access to objects, which can over time cause entanglement of data access permissions. This, however, does not mean that Snowflake automatically ensures a scalable and easy-to-maintain access control structure, and as we will see, architecting data access in Snowflake has different methods; not all of them fit every organization and every use case.

Snowflake's role-based access control applies both for data access and for actions performed. As an example, certain roles may be allowed to create objects (such as views), delete data, or update data while others will not.

6.2.1. Snowflake Security Model

Before we dive down into how users are authorized to data in Snowflake, let's first understand the objects in Snowflake, which would give us the high-level understanding needed for when we discuss authentication and authorization.

In Snowflake, there are the following objects defined:

- **Users** – Which can be either human users or application users. Some access definitions can be set in the scope of a user. For example, a user can be configured to log in only from specific IP addresses (see network security), or only using a specific authentication method (e.g., only using multifactor authentication). For more information about that, refer to the relevant chapters regarding authentication and network access control.

- **Roles** – Which define a set of privileges and are used by users. Each user can be granted one or more roles but may use only a single role per action performed.

- **Privileges** – Which are directives, specifying that a certain role can perform a certain action (e.g., SELECT, UPDATE, or CREATE USER) on a certain securable object.

- **Securable objects** – Which are the objects to which we are setting access. These include data objects (databases, schemas, tables, and views), but also other objects, such as roles, users, functions, file formats, stages, and sequences.

Snowflake's authorization is RBAC, meaning that the privileges are assigned to roles, and the users can perform the actions allowed to them according to the roles they own (or more specifically, the specific role they are using when performing the action).

This is quite different from other databases. For example, in Google BigQuery, when you are performing an action (such as sending a query), you have a mapping of the permissions that are granted to you based on the roles that were assigned to you or the groups you belong to in Google Cloud's Identity and Access Management. You don't need to decide which role to use for your query. Your access is the sum of the permissions granted to all your roles and identities.

In most databases (such as PostgreSQL), you are getting access that is granted to your user or to one of the groups you belong to. However, in Snowflake, you can specifically choose a certain role (one that you're granted with) for each action you perform. You can try to query a table with a certain role, get an error message stating that you don't have sufficient permissions, and then try with another role and succeed. This has its advantages and disadvantages, but is important to be aware of.

In addition, you may create a role hierarchy in Snowflake, meaning that a role will inherit the privileges from another role (which may, in turn, inherit privileges from other roles and so on). More on role hierarchies further in this chapter.

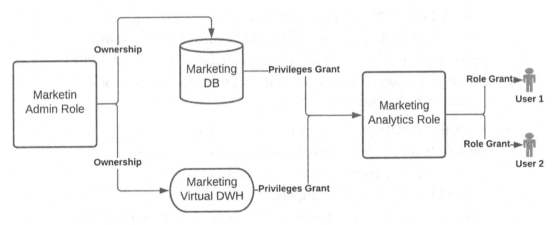

In this figure, there is a marketing admin role, which owns both the marketing database and the marketing virtual data warehouse. The owner then grants certain privileges to the marketing analytics role, such as usage of the data warehouse, database, and schema, and selects on the tables. The marketing analytics role is then granted to user 1 and user 2. Now, they can use this role to query data from the database. This can be, and in real life is, much more complicated than that, as users often have several roles, and these roles have a larger set of privileges.

6.2.2. The Built-In Roles in Snowflake

Snowflake comes out of the box with the following roles:

- **PUBLIC** – This role is granted to all users and, as such, should only be granted with objects you're comfortable with all of your users being able to access. Sometimes, objects get accidentally granted to the public role, which we should monitor (refer to Chapter 7, "Auditing and Monitoring," for this).

- **SYSADMIN** – This role should be used to manage all non-user and non-role objects in the account (databases, tables, views, etc., with the exception of objects specifically granted only to the ACCOUNTADMIN role). In addition, the best practice is to grant all custom roles to the SYSADMIN roles, so they can manage access to all underlying objects.

- **USERADMIN** – This role should be used only for the creation of users and roles. As a best practice, this role should be the only one used for creating users, so that it is easier to monitor user creation activities.

- **SECURITYADMIN** – This role should be able to manage all grants to objects in your Snowflake account. In addition, it should be able to perform user and role creation, as it is granted with the USERADMIN role. This role should be reserved only for grants management and should not be granted to any other role.

- **ACCOUNTADMIN** – This role has both the SYSADMIN and SECURITYADMIN roles granted to it and as such is a "superuser." In addition, some special privileges are only granted to the ACCOUNTADMIN role. It is important not to ever grant the ACCOUNTADMIN role to any other role, as this role is reserved to be the top-level role (same as a root account), and granting it to another role may create non-monitored security issues, as well as operational problems. It shouldn't be used for day-to-day administration, rather the lesser admin roles should be used for them.

- **ORGADMIN** – This role is (at the time of writing) not given by default, but only if you choose to self-manage your organization's accounts, and can create new accounts, as well as modify account settings.

You should monitor usage of all administrative roles (more in Chapter 7, "Auditing and Monitoring"). Likewise, you should only grant them to users who actually need them, as they have strong privileges that can be abused or can cause other issues. Specifically, such roles should not be used for actual data analysis (as this will be a breach of the separation of duties principle). In addition to that, you should never define an administrative role (especially ACCOUNTADMIN) as the default role of a user.

6.3. Designing Your Role Architecture

Before we begin, we think that this section is an especially important section. I suggest you take some time after reading it to reflect on optimal ways to architect data access in your organization. There is no one solution that fits all organizations, as managing access has a lot to do with the nature of the data stored, the general security policies in the organization, the preferences between leniency and strictness, and the amount of operational overhead which is reasonable to spend when managing data access.

In the end, in many cases, it will be *your* responsibility as a data engineer or administrator to enable users' access to data, and choosing a model that doesn't work well for your organization can have some dire security consequences, such as unintended data exposure, data breaches, but also compliance violations and operational issues like slowing down the organization's "time to value" and taking a large portion of the data administrator's time. This may sound grim, but you can look at this in the opposite direction – managing data access in a way that *is* suited well for your organization will help to be both secure and efficient.

Another word of advice, don't be quick to disqualify a certain approach just because someone says it's an anti-pattern. Eventually, it will be up to you to understand the needs of your organization and provide the best way to manage access to data.

6.3.1. Document Your Role Architecture

Once you make decisions about the data access architecture, we recommend putting the strategy in writing, in a document. The document should explain the role structure and hierarchy (if there is one), the processes for getting access to more data, as well as the access revocation process. The document would ideally be agreed as a protocol between the different stakeholders – data, security, privacy and governance, data owners, and data consumers.

Having a clear access policy helps reduce friction between the different stakeholders, but more importantly, it helps in maintaining consistency, which is important when you want to avoid a mess in the data access model of your organization.

6.3.2. Privilege Granting

In Snowflake, you can grant privileges to roles, and when doing that, you can use the optional parameter WITH GRANT OPTION, which means that not only are you granting the privilege, but you are granting the option for users with the specified granted role to grant the privilege to other roles.

The idea behind this is to enable self-management of roles and decentralize role granting. However, this can backfire, when users who are not proficient with the privileges and role structure in Snowflake, or with security and compliance requirements, are granting unwanted privileges.

That is why, whenever you are using this feature, do it in an organized way. For example, if your organization has data stewards in certain teams who are capable of granting such privileges within their part of the organization, and will do so with the specific privileges needed for a certain project, it may be good to do so. However, default to not allowing users to be able to do so, especially on large scales, where things can become messy.

An additional way of limiting object grants is to create schemas with the parameter WITH MANAGED ACCESS. When you're creating managed schemas, all objects within the schema can only be granted by the schema owner, not by the individual object owners. The advantage is that it reduces the amount of privileges being granted in an uncontrolled manner.

6.3.3. Approaches to Access Management

Let's discuss several ways to architect your data access. For each model, we will discuss the process required to access data, as well as the advantages and disadvantages. Note that your role management model has to suit *your* organization, so borrowing principles from several models to fit your usage is perfectly okay, provided that there's good logic behind that.

IdP-Dominated Access

In an IdP-dominated access model, the organization relies as much as possible on roles provisioned from the identity provider. That means that you limit the roles you're creating directly on Snowflake and instead inherit the roles from IdP groups. The logic behind that is that by unifying roles in a role-based access control data warehouse with their business context (the group from the IdP), you keep things tidy.

If, for example, there is a new employee in ACME Candies' finance department, they will be assigned to that group in ACME's IdP. This will automatically enable access to the new employee to all the data resources available to the finance department. This also has the potential of lowering the amount of time spent by data engineers on setting Snowflake roles and granting them to users.

There are, however, a few caveats to having a *purely* IdP-dominated data access control. This is usually good for when there are very blunt borders between the different roles, for example, when a certain identity group has a correlating database, schema, or at least a set of tables. This is not always the situation in all organizations.

It is also not solving for a need for temporary access to data (if a data scientist in ACME Candies requires access to marketing data, adding them to the marketing identity group can have other unintended consequences, such as granting them access to other marketing resources they should not have access to outside of Snowflake).

In addition, in many companies, the identities are managed by a team in IT, and getting an identity group added is often a process that starts with opening a ticket and continues with getting approval from the person's manager, as well as the owner of the group, who is not always the person who knows what the data access implications are and what project the data is needed for. This often creates a "ticket thread" with back and forth explanations and more people dragged into the process.

Lastly, this will mostly not solve for nonhuman users, who are in most cases configured as "regular" Snowflake users.

Classic Snowflake Role Management

An alternative to overreliance on IdP groups as roles is to create either functional or grouped by business unit roles in Snowflake. These roles will, sometimes, be cross-department, as needed. For example, the data scientists in ACME Candies may require a role that will allow them access both to sales and marketing data. This can be a specific role for data scientists allowing them access to both marketing and sales (which may be done by a hierarchy; see "Role Hierarchy" section later).

This also means that it will be easier to set access limited to only a subset of the users for a subset of the data. For example, if there are 200 data scientists in ACME Candies, and only a specific team needs access to specific data, it may make sense to provide them with a specific role for that data. This especially makes sense when the specific data has sensitive data in it, and you want to limit the exposure to the sensitive data as much as possible.

One downside about managing everything around your roles directly in Snowflake is that it may become an operational pain to maintain, as instead of IT tickets, the organization will now have to open a ticket with data engineering to allow access to a specific dataset, which may trigger a workflow of authorizations by the data owners or may just mean a lot of overhead for the data engineering teams.

Another downside is that if not kept according to a specific method, this may cause the role structure to become entangled, as more and more subsets are added to Snowflake by data engineers (as well as by data consumers if they're allowed to grant access on their own).

In addition, it is rare that anyone opens a ticket to revoke access they requested. This may lead to overprivileged data access, which may become a growing security and compliance risk.

Per Project Roles

Another use for custom Snowflake roles is for specific projects. For example, when ACME Candies has a new project to have a lychee-eggplant-flavored bubble gum, and this project requires data crunching by several teams in R&D, marketing, data science, and more, a role can be created specifically for this project, so that once the project is done (hopefully without any lychee-eggplant-flavored bubble gums produced), the role will be revoked. Additionally, if users are no longer part of the project, they can be revoked from the project.

This means that the custom Snowflake roles can have a higher granularity than just the business units and can be cross-team, but also sub-teams (not all marketing, R&D, or data science will have access to the lychee-eggplant project).

Role Per User

This is not a common practice, but we've seen it being designed in some organizations, either as a solution for the majority of data consumers or just to solve edge cases (more common).

When it happens, sometimes it's because of architects coming from a per user access control (which is common in many databases), and they're trying to replicate the same here.

The idea behind assigning a role per user is that it gives a very high level of granularity in data access, according to each specific use. If Timothy needs access to a specific table and Doron, working with him in the same team, does not, we will enable access only for Timothy.

The main problem with that approach, as you can guess, is that this gets harder to manage, especially in scale. That's what role-based access control is good for – to eliminate such overhead of setting access per user. When a new user onboards, the process in these cases is to give them a role that is replicated from a similar person, or open up access as they require it. The potential of making mistakes is big, as well as the potential for a lot of mundane work of the data administrators of granting and revoking access to all these users.

Functional Roles Coupled with Access Roles

In this model, you assign roles in your organization (mostly by using IdP provisioning) according to functional roles. For example: Claris is a "Financial Planner". These roles in Snowflake maps to sets of access roles, and these roles are granted to the functional role. And so, if a user is a part of the certain IdP functional group, they automatically are granted with the access mapped to that functional role.

In many organizations this is a good balance between hierarchy and keeping authorization simple. The downside is that this is still not very granular, and does not solve the problem of a certain user who needs access to specific resources of another group.

Role Hierarchy

Snowflake features a hierarchical role model. What this means is that you can not only grant roles to users but also to other roles. This gives great flexibility when architecting roles and can eliminate some of the overhead required when managing roles at scale and help reduce overprivileges given to users. It can also backfire and further complicate your data access management (see the following section "Hierarchy Hell").

Granting roles to other roles is pretty straightforward. You use the SQL command **GRANT**. In the following example, we are granting our SDR_LATAM team with the privileges of the SDR_GENERIC role:

```
GRANT ROLE SDR_GENERIC TO ROLE SDR_LATAM;
```

Hierarchical roles work especially well in certain situations. One is when you want to give access to common objects to a number of different teams. Let's consider an example where the different R&D teams in ACME are working on new candy flavors, and though the data about the different projects are only accessible by the respective teams, there is also a shared schema with generic information available to all of them, such as the raw materials' costs.

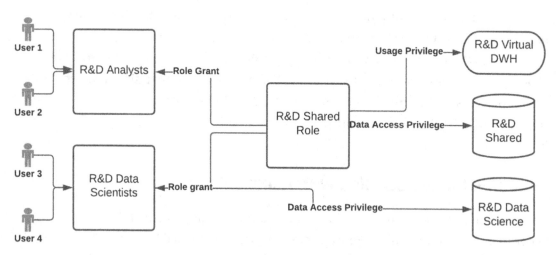

In this figure, you can see two R&D roles for two different teams (analysts and data scientists). These are probably provisioned by IdP, so when a new user is joining such a team, they automatically get granted that role. Both of these roles are granted with the R&D shared role, which gives them data access to shared R&D data, as well as to use the R&D virtual data warehouse. In addition to those shared objects, the data scientist role is also granted with data access privileges to other resources. In that way, additional teams can all get access to the shared objects, as well as to specific objects.

Another good use case for hierarchical roles would be when there is a temporary project which is cross-team and where data should be available to several different teams for the project's duration. Without hierarchical roles, this would mean editing all involved teams, granting them access to the different objects (tables, views, etc.). With hierarchical roles, you can set one role with the privileges configured and grant that role to the teams involved in the project. As an example, when ACME is working on their yearly Halloween candies project, this requires temporary access to different tables for many teams. This is done using a Project Halloween role, which is granted to the different teams as in the following example.

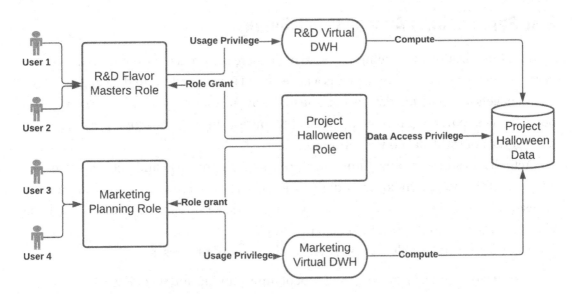

As you can see in this figure, two organizational roles, one from R&D and one from marketing, are granted with the role Project Halloween, which is granted with data access privileges to the data objects. Since they're using their team role, it also has access to other data objects which they can join, and each team can even use its own virtual data warehouse when accessing the data. As soon as the project is over, and Project Halloween is revoked, all teams automatically lose access to the data.

Hierarchy Hell

Role hierarchy is a double-edged sword and can become a complicating factor instead of a simplifying one. When you grant access of a role to another role, you may not realize that this role also inherits privileges from another role which are not needed by the role, and you are giving the assignee role with more privileges that it needs, thus increasing the risk. Likewise, when removing privileges from a role, you may be rightfully intimidated by the possibility that an inheriting role needs this privilege and will be affected, causing an operational issue.

Hierarchical roles can be hurting the opacity of your role hierarchy, and so, they need to be used sparingly and in a very clear way. In addition, try to refrain from creating a too high-tiered hierarchical structure, where you will need to recursively check a large number of roles to find out the actual privileges of a user or a role.

Self-Service: Data Access Provisioning

In many organizations managing access to data, there is a process established where a person who seeks access to data opens a ticket with IT, or directly with data engineering, and then gets access to the data, according to the organization's policies. This can depend on certain things like the requester identity, business justification provided, managerial approval, data owner approval, etc.

Actually, in some organizations, such processes do not exist, and decisions are ad hoc. In this case, our recommendations are to start with creating such clear data access policies so that decisions are consistent and make sure data is available to those who need it while not creating too high of a risk.

There are several problems with such "rubber stamp" processes:

- Data engineers are spending a lot of time granting and revoking access to data (because they're the ones who *can* do it), instead of doing more productive things.

- This entails in many cases a delay to the availability of data for the consumers.

- In certain cases, this pressure can even degrade security when data is granted not according to policies because corners are cut when the data engineering teams are "under attack" by many data consumers who want access. They may give too broad access just to streamline the process.

In such cases, it makes sense to allow self-service access to data, based on such processes. There are several ways to do this; let's discuss them.

Role Creation Delegation

The discretionary data access model in Snowflake allows users to grant access to roles, and not just a centralized team; this can be done by delegating data access granting to the data owners within Snowflake. This means that you can give role owners the ability to grant other users with that role and so de-centralize the access management.

There are several issues with this, making it unpopular in organizations. Not all data owners have sufficient knowledge in Snowflake outside of querying data, and not in all cases it makes sense to teach them how to do that (they do have their "day jobs" as well).

Building a Self-Service Portal

For certain organizations, it makes sense to not only provision users and groups but also to provision data access by using an application. This is done by creating an application that supports workflows that automates access to data. As an example, the application can enable users to request access to certain schemas or databases, which triggers a workflow that ends up in approving the access. A daemon process can then revoke the temporary access after a certain amount of time.

This means that at the end of the day, the organization has a data marketplace, which allows it to make data available easily and in a transparent manner, while not breaking compliance and reducing risks, as whenever a user requests access to data, the request is audited, and if needed, the workflow may require authorizations from business owners.

In some organizations, this self-service application may even contain the option to create new data objects by data owners. In such cases, the application acts as a wrapper around the Snowflake, and using it is using it as a platform to set up new ingestion pipelines and then to assign privileges for data consumers to use the data.

The main downside of this approach is the investment involved in setting up such a service and making sure that it remains up to date. However, such self-service portals can allow users to log in to a wrapper application, where they can see available datasets. This can either be built on top of the private data exchange listings (see Chapter 8, "Secure Data Sharing with Snowflake," for that) or built based on privilege grants.

Let's say that in ACME Candies, the customer support department offers temporary self-service access to a database of support data they think may be helpful to other teams as well. When a user logs into the application, they can request access to the dataset. This may trigger some sort of a process inside the organization, with or without the need for an approval, but the result will be that the provisioning application will send Snowflake the following command:

GRANT ROLE cs_shared **TO ROLE** <user_team_role>;

This application can even have a service that runs periodically and revokes those temporary grants. There are several ways to implement this – temporarily granting the privileges themselves to the user's team role or giving the user a temporary role with the needed privileges. Keep in mind that assigning a new role may not be the best option as the user will not be able to join the data with other data they have access to from other roles or use another data warehouse.

Third-Party Solutions

There are third-party solutions that can integrate with Snowflake to provide data access management. These vendor solutions come in several flavors which have their advantages and disadvantages and either orchestrate setting of privileges in Snowflake or perform the data access control on the network level.

The main advantage of using such tools is that you can have a more rich set of access control abilities such as attribute-based access control (ABAC) or even self-service access control, without having to build and especially maintain such complexities.

In many cases, these third-party solutions also provide the same enhanced functionality for other (non-Snowflake) data environments, so you can have a clear data access strategy across different data stores. The downside is that these services incur additional costs.

6.3.4. Creating Your Own Blend of Data Access

The previous list of data access options should not make you a fanatic. We hope that you've seen that each model has its advantages and disadvantages and that in many cases you don't want to go with only one solution. It is more than okay to do cherry picking and create a more elaborate plan that treats certain parts of your data in one way and others in another.

For example, you may decide to have your data separated into sensitive and nonsensitive data (if that even makes sense for your organization) and have a more strict access control model on the sensitive data, while using a more loose model on the nonsensitive data.

A good example of a balanced approach is to give functional roles to users based on their organizational roles and then attach specific "building block" roles to these roles.

6.4. Fine-Grained Data Access Control

So far we've dealt with access to securable objects. In Snowflake, that means that we assign access down to the database, schema, or table level, but in several cases, we want to be even more granular than that and authorize or restrict access to parts of the data. We may give access to a specific table to a set of roles, but restrict access to specific columns or rows only for a subset of these roles.

In this section, we will discuss the cases where it makes sense to have a more fine-grained access control and how to set it up.

6.4.1. Column-Based Access Control

You may encounter this also as column-based security, column-level access control, or column-level security. Sometimes, this comes as a requirement to mask data based on columns. Whatever it is called, in the technical level, it means that you have certain tables where different people can access different columns, according to their needs or access level. In most cases, this is due to the types of data stored in different columns, which map to groups of people who are eligible to access such types of data.

For example, a table may contain a lot of information about the employees in ACME Candies, and you want to allow only HR employees access to certain details (such as employee ratings); only a certain team should be able to access employees' bank account details so they can deposit their salaries, while the employees themselves can update their contact information.

In databases, there are several approaches to column-level security. In some platforms, you can set access permissions at the column level (in the same way you grant access to a table, you grant access to specific columns). In Snowflake, the access control mechanism's most granular object is a table (or a view), so you can't set access to specific columns only. You can, however, create column-level security in other ways, as we will see here.

It is important to note that there are several ways to go about when redacting the data. Data can be completely deleted, but it may also be masked. As we will see, masking data gives better flexibility of removing parts of the data to retain more data processing value, while still anonymizing data. For example, the data scientists in ACME Candies should not see the personal details (such as customer names) of candy tasters, but when they process data, they may want to get a hash (unique identifier) of the taster's identity, so they can make data analytics with relevancy for the unique tasters (to know each taster's results across the data, without knowing their true identity). In the same way, perhaps ACME wants them to have access only to the phone number prefix (as it indicates the region), but not to the complete phone number.

Let's discuss ways to achieve column-level security, as some of them have advantages over others, and which one you will implement depends on the exact problems you're trying to solve and the scale of your operations.

Static Cloning of Data

An obvious way to give users a subset of the data is to create copies of the data, with redacted information, suited for the different people accessing the data. This means that per our example, HR will get a table with the employee details containing the employee ratings, accounting will get a copy with the bank account details, and so on. The rest of the data can either be copied, masked, or not copied at all. That means that the tables may retain the exact same schema, with redacted data, or get tables with fewer columns.

To do so, the traditional way of anonymizing data is to create several copies of the same data and allow access to the tables containing the data with the sensitivity level which correlates with the users' access level. The data is traditionally copied by ETL processes, to different locations, where the access controls are placed. There are several ways to do so in Snowflake, including using tasks.

The upside is that this may create a very clear separation between different versions of the data. Objects clear for a certain access level may be placed in a certain location (database or schema) to make the borderline between different levels of anonymization very clear. However, this approach has several disadvantages.

It is usually done in intervals, and the freshness of the data is updated accordingly. For example, if the ETL process is daily, the teams accessing the anonymized copies are getting stale data. This may or may not be crucial to your operations, depending on the business use case. If it does not require up-to-date data, this is not a deal breaker.

This method is intensive on data writing. This means that once you set up such copies of the data, they are created whether or not the data is needed. This is also true to the storage used (though in Snowflake this is not a major expense). This means that this method is by design better for situations where there are intensive reads of the data, but writing the data is okay to be in intervals.

The third disadvantage is that it creates a lot of copies of data (each table can have several duplications to different teams, and there may be a large number of such tables). In addition to the storage costs, this creates problems when you want to retroactively change anonymization levels (e.g., consider an audit that says that a certain anonymization is not good enough) and may grow to situations where the whereabouts of data start to be messy.

Finally, someone needs to write and maintain the ETLs, which – depending on the complexity and amount of different types of data and number of duplications needed – may add overhead to the data engineering teams.

As a result of these disadvantages, the usage of static copies of data is often not the best choice. However, in certain situations, it may still be valid, and the conditions are intensive reading, freshness of the data not being a major issue, and that you perform this in a way that is still organized and governed. The latter condition often means that it works better for a smaller number of tables.

Some of the disadvantages of static copies of the data can be negated if instead of creating actual copies of the data, you create an abstraction by using views. That means that instead of actually copying the data to other tables, you create a view that filters the data per the restrictions you want to put in place.

This eliminates the need for writing ETL, as the logic of the data redaction moves to the views. It also means that the data is fresh, as it is pulled from the underlying tables. That means that in most use cases, it is a preferred way over copying data (making this an ELT, rather than an ETL).

Another point to consider is that when you're cloning data, it is the ability to perform k-anon anonymization. This means anonymizing items according to minimal item group sizes that enables de-anonymization of data. This is a less straightforward process that can be done on data, converting it to an anonymized table. Snowflake also has such a capability in development (at the time of writing) that enables it to create an anonymized view from a table, with a k-anon anonymization level based on a group size provided by the user. The result is planned to be such a statement that will anonymize the table:

```
// Anonymize purchases table into the anonymized_purchases view, with a k of 7
CALL SYSTEM$ANONYMIZE('purchases', 'anonymized_purchases', 7)
```

Abstraction by Using Secure Views

An even more dynamic way than by using views to create virtual duplicated tables is using views to dynamically serve different data according to the user requesting the data or, more commonly, according to their role. In this case, we will check the identity of the data consumer with functions such as CURRENT_USER(), CURRENT_ROLE(), or IS_ROLE_IN_SESSION() and perform the logic accordingly.

This way we can check whether the user is a part of a certain IdP group (as long as it's propagated from the IdP to Snowflake, see Chapter 4, "Authentication: Keeping Strangers Out," for information about that). Whenever someone has a certain role (or lacks a certain role), we can give them a different value for a certain column.

When doing this, we recommend using secure views over regular views. A secure view is a Snowflake-specific type of view that has two additional features to a regular view. The first is that the user can't read the view definition (unless the user is the owner of the secure view), which may be better to conceal the exact logic according to which you limit access to sensitive data. The second is that it cancels certain optimizations used by Snowflake, through which users can infer values which they don't have access to.

As an example, let's say that there's a single table where ACME Candies stores employee details. However, based on the role of the user accessing the data, they would like to give different results. Let's first set a mock employee's table and fill it with mock data:

```
CREATE TABLE employees_table (
  employee_id integer,
  employee_name text,
  home_address text,
  home_phone text,
  salary integer,
  evaluation integer
);
```

```
INSERT INTO employees_table VALUES
(1, 'Karl Herz', '27 West Street', '555-6655', 999999, 1000),
(2, 'Anna Lytics', '26 West Street', '555-5566', 999999, 1000);
```

Next, let's create three roles for this exercise – HR, accounting, and office admin:

```
CREATE ROLE OFFICEADMIN;
CREATE ROLE ACCOUNTING;
CREATE ROLE HR;
```

Finally, let's create a secure view, which returns results from the source employees_table table, depending on the role you are using:

```
CREATE SECURE VIEW v_employees AS
SELECT employee_id, employee_name,
/* Administration specific columns: */
CASE
```

```sql
    WHEN current_role() IN ('OFFICEADMIN') THEN
        home_address
    ELSE
    ''
  END AS home_address,
CASE
    WHEN current_role() IN ('OFFICEADMIN') THEN
        home_phone
    ELSE
    ''
  END AS home_phone,
/* Accounting specific columns: */
CASE
    WHEN current_role() IN ('ACCOUNTING') THEN
        salary
    ELSE
    0
  END AS salary,
/* HR specific columns: */
CASE
    WHEN current_role() IN ('HR') THEN
        evaluation
    ELSE
    0
  END AS evaluation
  FROM employees_table;
```

As you can see here, you are getting dynamic results, based on the CURRENT_ROLE() function. You can customize this by adding more roles to the in clause or adding additional conditions. This technique can even be used when sharing data across accounts, where the CURRENT_ACCOUNT() can determine what columns you will be getting (more on that in Chapter 8, "Secure Data Sharing with Snowflake").

Dynamic Masking

Dynamic masking is a feature released especially for configuring column-level security in Snowflake. At the time of writing, it is enabled for enterprise accounts and above. With dynamic masking, you create masking policies, which are describing the transformations you want to apply to data. You then assign these masking policies to the columns containing the data you want to apply anonymization on.

If dynamic masking resembles the previous method of abstraction by using secure views, it is because that's what it is. Behind the scenes, dynamic masking is a further abstraction of secure views, and whenever you implement column access policies, Snowflake uses secure views to implement the logic which serves different content to different data consumers.

The advantage over creating the abstraction layer of views on your own is in the reusability of the policies, which also means easier maintenance over time. In addition, when you apply new masking logic on tables, there is no need to create a new object, assign privileges to it, and instruct the data users to query it instead of the original table (though this can be skipped by setting the view to the same name of the original table and renaming the original table instead, but this often creates additional complications in an already operational infrastructure).

The disadvantages are that you need an enterprise account, and in case the access control logic consists of more than just column-based security, the logic may be more easily represented in self-made secure views (or, in case you want to apply column- and row-based access controls, you may want to use dynamic masking with row access policies, as per the following section).

Here's an example of setting up a dynamic masking policy and applying it. We will apply the same transformations we applied in the secure view example previously, so in case you skipped here, first create the table and roles per the earlier example. Now, let's create the masking policies:

```
CREATE MASKING POLICY emp_contact AS (val string) RETURNS string ->
  CASE
    WHEN CURRENT_ROLE() IN ('OFFICEADMIN') THEN val
    ELSE ''
  END;
```

```
CREATE MASKING POLICY emp_financial AS (val integer) RETURNS integer ->
  CASE
    WHEN CURRENT_ROLE() IN ('ACCOUNTING') THEN val
    ELSE 0
  END;

CREATE MASKING POLICY emp_hr AS (val integer) RETURNS integer ->
  CASE
    WHEN CURRENT_ROLE() IN ('HR') THEN val
    ELSE 0
  END;
```

We are creating these three policies – one to handle contact details, one to handle financial details, and one to handle HR-related details. Of course in a real-world scenario, we might set one for emails, one for social security number, etc. Now, let's apply these policies:

```
ALTER TABLE employees_table MODIFY COLUMN home_address SET MASKING POLICY
emp_contact;
ALTER TABLE employees_table MODIFY COLUMN home_phone SET MASKING POLICY
emp_contact;
ALTER TABLE employees_table MODIFY COLUMN salary SET MASKING POLICY
emp_financial;
ALTER TABLE employees_table MODIFY COLUMN evaluation SET MASKING POLICY
emp_hr;
```

At this point, you may be thinking to yourself that this is not saving a lot of time over doing the same using a secure view. However, the benefits are that you don't need to have a view for each filtered table, and once you create policies, you can apply them on multiple tables easily. In addition, as a built-in feature, it can be monitored and governed better, which we will see in Chapter 7, "Auditing and Monitoring."

Another relevant issue around dynamic masking you may want to be aware of is a feature which was announced but not released yet (at the time of writing) called conditional masking. Conditional masking allows you to mask a certain column, based on the value of other columns. For example, it may mask all names from certain regions or mask phone numbers of people defined as customers, but not for employees.

Column-Based Security for Semi-structured Data

In certain conditions, you may want to limit access based on semi-structured locations of data (using the term "column" broadly in this context). For example, ACME may have a JSON containing test results as part of a table, and this semi-structured data contains fields which should be available only to certain users or roles.

When we want to implement access control over semi-structured data, things can get more complicated than on regular columns. Here's how to implement it as part of a view abstraction, and here's how to implement it in dynamic masking.

Let's assume that there is a table with extra employee details that needs to be masked, because they have the past evaluations of the employees. Let's first create the mock table and add some data to it:

```
CREATE TABLE employee_extra_details (employee_id integer, details variant);
INSERT INTO employee_extra_details (employee_id, details)
SELECT 1, PARSE_JSON('{"hobbies": ["hiking", "food"], "last_evaluation": 100}');
```

Now, let's create the transformation function. This function takes the JSON content and edits here:

```
CREATE OR REPLACE FUNCTION get_masked_extra_details(v variant)
RETURNS variant
LANGUAGE javascript
AS
'
V["last_evaluation"] = -1;
return V;
';
```

We can now create the dynamic policy that uses this function:

```
CREATE OR REPLACE MASKING POLICY data_mask_variant AS (val variant) RETURNS
variant ->
CASE WHEN CURRENT_ROLE() IN ('HR') THEN val
ELSE get_masked_extra_details(val)
END;
```

And finally apply it:

```
ALTER TABLE employee_extra_details
MODIFY COLUMN details
SET MASKING POLICY data_mask_variant;
```

As you can see

1. You can apply the same on a secure view, with the same comments we made about using a secure view vs. using a dynamic view.

2. Dynamic masking of semi-structured data, especially when it is not constant in its format, can be a challenging task.

De-tokenization and Decryption

An advanced use case of dynamic masking, which can also be applied using secure views, is to use a dynamic masking to de-tokenize or decrypt data, based on certain roles which are querying the data. When doing so, the data is either kept encrypted, or a token of the data is being kept in Snowflake. When querying the data, if a certain condition is met (e.g., the role PRIVATE_DATA_ENABLED), the dynamic masking policy calls an external function that decrypts or de-tokenizes the data in the specific column or columns.

6.4.2. Row-Based Access Control

Whereas column-based access control deals with limiting access to certain columns, which is done mainly to restrict access to certain types of data containing sensitive information, row-based access control limits access to specific rows within tables. There are several use cases where such requirements come into play, such as

1. **Regional separation** – Where you want to restrict access to certain records based on the region of each record. An example of this is due to privacy requirements, which requires placing access control restrictions over access to information on data subjects of specific locations (such as the EU).

2. **A multi-tenant environment** – Where certain tables contain data which should be limited when retrieved to different tenants using the data.

3. **Team-based data ownership** – An example we've seen is in financial institutions, where there are analyst teams who should only be allowed to view details of specific customers. This often also requires some sort of hierarchy, where certain roles should have access to several analyst teams' data.

Sometimes, such row-level security is implemented by an application accessing the data, but in terms of security, it is always better to have a defense-in-depth approach and apply the access restrictions in the data infrastructure layer as well.

Implementing Row-Level Security Static Copies

Similar to column-based security, one approach is to separate subsets of the data in the tables to multiple locations, based on the row-level logic. That means that if you have teams based on countries, you will either store the data according to such restrictions from the get-go or will create the separation later on. You can use Snowflake tasks to perform the ETL tasks of creating the copies of the data containing only the required rows or use secure views to give such access.

The advantages of this, in a simple case, can be that there are very clear boundaries between the different "regions." If, as an example, only EU employees of ACME should be able to access EU customers' data, you can set them up with an appropriate IdP group which will be propagated to Snowflake, and only this role will have access to the customers_eu table.

The disadvantage of this is that when things get complicated, the maintenance required with making all these duplications can backfire and can leave you with a messy database, which can lead to security issues as well as to a lot of data engineering resources spent on this, especially when there are a lot of subgroups, tables, and changes to the data schemas, users, and roles.

In addition, if the data is totally separated, getting data about the entire dataset can prove difficult (e.g., when a team needs to produce global reports). This is another example of why it's important to understand the requirements from the different teams, to make the correct data access decisions.

Implementing Row-Level Security Using Secure Views

A more dynamic approach would be to use secure views, which will contain the filtering logic according to the row-level security requirements. This will be done dynamically, based on the user or role used to pull the data. The user will query the view, instead of querying the underlying table, which will filter only the relevant rows.

First, let's create a sales table, with some mock data, to show regional sales for ACME Candies:

```
CREATE TABLE sales_summary (sale_id integer, tcv integer, acv integer,
customer_name text, region_id integer);
INSERT INTO sales_summary (sale_id, tcv, acv, customer_name, region_id)
VALUES
(1, 333, 111, 'User 1', 1),
(2, 333, 111, 'User 2', 2),
(3, 333, 111, 'User 3', 1),
(4, 333, 111, 'User 4', 3),
(5, 333, 111, 'User 5', 3),
(6, 333, 111, 'User 6', 2);
```

Now, let's create a mapping table, showing the regional entitlement of each role:

```
CREATE TABLE rows_filtering_by_regions (role_name text, region_id integer);
INSERT INTO rows_filtering_by_regions (role_name, region_id) VALUES
('REGION2', 2);
```

Finally, let's create the secure view, with the logic to filter the results based on the users' roles:

```
CREATE SECURE VIEW v_sales_summary AS
SELECT sale_id, tcv, acv, customer_name, region_id
FROM sales_summary
WHERE region_id IN (
  SELECT region_id FROM rows_filtering_by_regions
  WHERE role_name=CURRENT_ROLE()
);
```

Now, only users accessing the data with the REGION2 role will be able to see sales in region 2.

We may want to make use of the CURRENT_AVAILABLE_ROLES() function instead, to allow us to see all results meeting any of the roles we have enabled to our users. In this case, even if we are not currently using REGION2 when accessing the data, we will see all results from our region. This also enables us to assign several regions (or other row-based filters) to the same user(s). This is our secure view in this case:

```
CREATE OR REPLACE SECURE VIEW v_sales_summary AS
SELECT sale_id, tcv, acv, customer_name, region_id
FROM sales_summary
WHERE region_id IN (
  SELECT region_id FROM rows_filtering_by_regions
  WHERE role_name IN (SELECT value FROM TABLE(flatten(input => parse_
json(CURRENT_AVAILABLE_ROLES())))))
);
```

Abstraction by Using Secure UDFs

Sometimes, you want to create an even more fine-grained access control by using secure functions instead of secure views. Secure functions, like secure views, are eliminating certain optimizations, preventing data guessing, and they also block non-owners from viewing their logic itself. The advantage of a secure function is that you can use them with parameters, to limit pulling the data by certain parameters.

For example, ACME Candies may create the following secure function that will be exposed from HR, to only respond if a certain employee exists in the database:

```
CREATE SECURE FUNCTION is_employee (employee_to_check string)
RETURNS BOOLEAN AS
'EXISTS (
SELECT 1 FROM employees_table
WHERE UPPER(employee_name) = UPPER(employee_to_check))';
```

Same can be applied for pulling complete tables based on row- and column-level security. More on secure functions can be found also in Chapter 8, "Secure Data Sharing with Snowflake."

Row-Level Security in Semi-structured Data

As with column-level security, things get a bit more complicated when semi-structured data is involved. This means that you will need to change the logic to filter according to certain conditions in the JSON element stored within the record. As an example, the operational teams may only be able to pull data with the "event_type" set to "operational" in a variant column.

Let's first create mock tables with some mock data. We'll create a soc_events table and a mapping table showing which role can access what event types:

```
CREATE TABLE soc_events (event_id integer, details variant);
INSERT INTO soc_events (event_id, details)
SELECT 1, PARSE_JSON('{"event_data": "some data goes here...", "event_type": "operational"}');
INSERT INTO soc_events (event_id, details)
SELECT 2, PARSE_JSON('{"event_data": "some data goes here...", "event_type": "non-operational"}');

CREATE TABLE soc_events_mapping (role string, event_type string);
INSERT INTO soc_events_mapping
VALUES ('OPERATIONS', 'operational');
```

Now, let's create the view, with the filtering logic:

```
CREATE SECURE VIEW v_soc_events AS
SELECT * FROM soc_events
WHERE details:"event_type" IN
(SELECT event_type FROM soc_events_mapping WHERE role = CURRENT_ROLE());
```

Finally, let's create the operations' role and grant it with access to the secure view:

```
CREATE ROLE operations;
GRANT USAGE ON DATABASE <DB> TO operations;
GRANT USAGE ON SCHEMA <DB>.<SCHEMA> TO operations;
GRANT USAGE ON <WAREHOUSE> TO ROLE operations;
GRANT SELECT ON VIEW v_soc_events TO ROLE operations;
GRANT ROLE operations TO USER <USER>;
```

Now, when we run the following query, we should get only the operational events:

```
USE operations;
SELECT * FROM v_soc_events;
```

Snowflake Row Access Policies

Instead of writing your own implementation of row-based security, you can use Snowflake's row access policies. Similar to dynamic masking, row access policies are created once and can be then applied on one or more tables or views. In this case, unlike dynamic masking, the policy defines the filtering to apply, so that users are getting rows from the table based on specific conditions.

For example, ACME Candies wants to allow access to the raw sales data based on the regional entitlement of the roles. We will create a mock raw sales data on which we will apply the policy and a mapping table, mapping the entitlement of the different regions to the roles.

First, let's create the mock data:

```
CREATE TABLE sales_raw (sales_info string, region string);
INSERT INTO sales_raw VALUES ('test', 'eu'), ('test2', 'us');

CREATE TABLE sales_entitlements (role_entitled string, region string);
INSERT INTO sales_entitlements VALUES ('SALES_EU', 'eu'), ('SALES_US', 'us');
```

Now, let's create the row access policy, which defines that if the requesting role is SALES_ADMIN, they will see all sales, regardless of region. However, other roles will be looked up in the mapping table, to check if the current role can view data from the specific region:

```
CREATE ROW ACCESS POLICY regional_access AS
(region_filter VARCHAR) RETURNS BOOLEAN ->
CURRENT_ROLE() = 'SALES_ADMIN'
OR EXISTS (
  SELECT 1 FROM sales_entitlements
  WHERE region = region_filter
  AND role_entitled = CURRENT_ROLE()
);
```

Now, what we do is apply the regional_access policy on the region column of sales_raw. This flexibility of applying the policy on a specific column (or columns) can help when in another table that column may be called item_region or customer_region instead of region. Here is the assignment command:

```
ALTER TABLE sales_raw ADD ROW ACCESS POLICY regional_access ON (region);
```

Some final notes on row access policies:

- Row access policies can also be applied on external tables, which can make secure data access faster, as it may reduce or eliminate ETLs needed to be done on such data.

- Row access policies and dynamic masking policies can work alongside each other.

- Row access policies (unlike secure views) also work when deleting or updating data.

Hierarchical Row-Level Security

As mentioned earlier, in certain situations, it makes sense to configure a hierarchical row-level security model. This solves for an organization where certain teams require access to specific rows, and "parent" teams need access to data of several of these teams' data. For example, in ACME Candies, there are regional account executive teams, and for each group of regions, there is a managing team that should have access to all the data within all their regions.

There are several ways to go about this. You can use Snowflake's built-in hierarchical role model and grant access of all privileges of the regional teams to the management team role, or you can add the hierarchy to the view abstraction layer itself. The way to do this depends on how you model your roles, which should be based on what will make sense and be the cleanest long-term way to maintain roles and entitlements.

6.4.3. Combining Column and Row Security

Having column-level security does not mean you don't need row-level security and vice versa. In fact, in many cases, we are blessed with the opportunity to implement both row-level security and column-level security on the same data. The good news is that you can do so quite easily, regardless of the way you choose to implement each restriction.

For example, dynamic masking can be applied on a view, so if you choose to implement row-level security by a view abstraction layer, you can then apply dynamic masking on its results. You can also implement both logics in the filtering done in the view level. Here's an example for that. Finally, and that would probably be the most tidy way in most scenarios, you can implement both as policies (dynamic masking and row access policies).

If there's one thing to stress here, it is to have these processes well documented within your organization, as they can become a sore spot for knowledge transfer and things not working, resulting in either giving too much access to data which increases security risks or creating an organizational bottleneck around, well, you (if you're the one setting up such permissions).

6.4.4. Attribute-Based Access Control

Snowflake does not officially have attribute-based access control (ABAC). This does not mean that you can't, at least partially, implement ABAC in Snowflake and set specific access control based on specific policies. As an example, if we want to create limitations over the tool which your users are using when accessing specific data, you can implement that using the CURRENT_CLIENT() context function.

As an example, in ACME Candies, customer success engineers are given a Snowflake user, but the security policy to be enforced is that they only access incident data from Snowflake's UI. To do that, let's assume we have an incidents table; we can create the following overlay view:

```
CREATE SECURE VIEW v_incidents AS
SELECT * FROM incidents
WHERE CURRENT_CLIENT() LIKE 'Snowflake UI%';
```

Now, if we grant the customer success team's role with access to v_incidents, the filter of the client type will always be applied, and only if it is Snowflake's UI, they will be able to query the data. This may also be combined with other restrictions, of course. However, when doing so, please remember that if these restrictions are not visible, they may come to haunt you when someone tries to query data and they fail for no obvious reason. You can preemptively look in the query and access log to understand the impact of such operations (for more information about those logs, refer to Chapter 7, "Auditing and Monitoring").

6.4.5. Self-Service Access Control

In certain cases, especially when the organization is mature in its data consumption, and has a large number of data consumers, and many different types of data, there arises a need for allowing self-service access to data. The logic behind this is that if we can automate the processes of authorizing data to data consumers, we can get data faster to its consumers (which translates to better value for the data, as time is often an important factor in such projects) and maintain the same level of security.

The process of allowing self-service to data consists of provisioning the data authorization by an external application that grants and revokes access to the data, according to certain workflows. In its simplest form, it's a replacement of something that data engineers are doing as a "rubber stamp." For example, if the process of authorizing data is that when the employee opens a ticket, gets approval from the data owner, and then a data engineer runs the grant access command, it can be automated without the need of the data engineer.

The main downside of such a system, which is also the reason why this is not the right solution for all organization sizes is that someone needs to develop the application and maintain it over time. In addition, it only makes sense to create such a system when there is enough structure and a clear process. If, for example, the self-service application "doesn't know" who the data owner is, if the process requires their approval, things will break.

6.4.6. Third-Party Solutions

As we've seen, there are different ways to set access to data in Snowflake, including fine-grained access control such as row-based and column-based security. There is a trade-off between the amount of security value you'll be getting and the amount of effort you will need to invest when setting things up and in ongoing maintenance.

However, another option is to use a third-party solution. These solutions add better data security and governance on top of Snowflake (and other data platforms). They usually give you better tools for managing roles, permissions, and fine-grained access control in scale and offer additional functionality. Such solutions will usually either handle the security on the Snowflake side by creating the different objects for you or perform the security as a network proxy.

6.5. Rolling Out Access Control Changes

In production systems, changes in code and configuration should be rolled out in a safe way. The world of software development is a bit more structured in that regard, and in database management, sometimes, there is a tendency to just apply configuration changes. It is important to attempt to be as methodical as possible in changes to access controls.

In your organization, we recommend that you set a process for access control changes, especially the more complicated ones mentioned earlier. If you're introducing new fine-grained access control which is a big leap, first apply them in testing and staging environments and let the relevant data consumers (analysts, data scientists, data accessing applications, etc.) work with the new access control model, to make sure that everything is working properly.

6.6. Summary

In this chapter, we discussed data access control or authorization to data. This is a very important topic in data security, and we hope that you enjoyed learning about the different ways you can balance between security and productivity. Building a model that works for your organization, is well documented, and is understood by the data consumers in the organization is at the heart of giving a secure data processing service. Using the tools in this chapter, you can probably find the most efficient way for your organization to operate in a clear role structure and use the tools needed to protect your data from unauthorized exposure.

CHAPTER 7

Auditing and Monitoring

An important part of security is visibility and logging. The ability to have an audit of the actions performed on the protected assets (in this case Snowflake) is important both from a compliance perspective and to mitigate security risks. The ability to monitor your Snowflake accounts allows you to focus your efforts around security and know when stuff needs attention or goes wrong.

You'd be happy to know that many parts of the work required with getting your auditing and monitoring up and running require little effort on your end.

Throughout this chapter, we've added examples that will help you get started in making value from the raw data that Snowflake offers. These examples, we hope, are enough to help you get started in setting up your own monitoring and auditing, as there are a lot of individual preferences when it comes to keeping track of security issues.

7.1. Snowflake Audits Characteristics

Before digging into the various metadata that you can acquire from Snowflake's views and functions, here are a couple of features that make auditing of Snowflake data easier than most equivalent platforms.

7.1.1. Every Operation Is Audited

Unlike other data warehouses, which in many cases require specifically configuring logging of access to the database, as well as logging of all queries running on the database, Snowflake logs both of these as an audit log. Not only does it log it, but the logging is retained for a significant period (up to one year). This does not require activating or configuring anything, such as a storage bucket to keep the logs.

As we've encountered cases where people asked themselves "where are the logs," only to find out that no logs were configured, this is a breath of fresh air.

109

© Ben Herzberg, Yoav Cohen 2022
B. Herzberg and Y. Cohen, *Snowflake Security*, https://doi.org/10.1007/978-1-4842-7389-0_7

7.1.2. Audits Are Available via… Snowflake

Not only are the logs working out of the box, but the logs are also very accessible, as you can query them as Snowflake views or table functions. This makes it easy for data engineering teams, who are using Snowflake themselves, to query the data quickly with SQL statements or to build dashboards on top of it.

7.2. Snowflake Metadata

The access logs and query logs are part of the metadata kept in Snowflake for your account objects and usage. Having both the logs and the configuration, in one place, enables you to perform analytics that can help you better adhere to security requirements and help you keep better track of relevant security issues, such as overprivileged users, access problems, and identify bad security practices.

7.2.1. Account Usage vs. Information Schema

Metadata views are accessible from two locations in Snowflake. One is the information_ schema schema that's available for each database in your Snowflake account, which we will refer to as "information schema" from now on. The other is the schema account_ usage, inside the database called Snowflake, that's available in all Snowflake accounts. While the information schema contains a more up-to-date configuration of the specific database, the account usage views contain delayed metadata logging. The data in the information schema is further divided into views and table functions.

The main differences between the metadata in the information schema and that in the account usage are as follows:

1. Data in the information schema views are up to date with the current configuration of your Snowflake account, while it takes a while for the data to appear in the account usage views. The time it takes depends on the specific view but is somewhere between 45 minutes and 3 hours. You can see the specific data latency per view in the documentation.

2.   The account usage data also contains data for dropped objects. This is of utmost importance for security auditing and monitoring, as we don't want to ignore objects which do not exist anymore.

3.   The retention time for historical data in the information schema is only between a week and six months (depending on the specific view). The retention time for account usage can be up to one year.

4.   Retrieving and processing data from the account_usage views may take a long time, even for relatively simple queries. In fact, if you are doing intensive analytics on the metadata, it might be a good idea to temporarily copy the data to separate tables.

You can view the full list of views, along with their retention time, and the information contained within each one of them in the documentation.

7.2.2. Relevant Views for Security in Snowflake.account_usage

Before digging in and looking at the data, we thought it would be good to give an overview of the views where you can find the most relevant information for security purposes. The following views are all in the account usage schema. Note that some of these views are more useful than others, and we will concentrate on them throughout this chapter, and there may be others with some security implications, but also with useful operational metadata that you can use to track metrics related to storage, costs, and more.

It is important to note that you need to use an ACCOUNTADMIN role to be able to query the SNOWFLAKE database metadata tables. As we already explained before, using the ACCOUNTADMIN should be used sparingly and mostly only to create other objects and assign privileges to roles. In this spirit, before we query the SNOWFLAKE database, we may want to either use one of the "lesser administrative roles" to access this database or have a dedicated role for accessing this database. In ACME Candies, the chosen role is log_analyzer, and so, as an ACCOUNTADMIN, let's create the new role and grant it with the required privileges:

```
CREATE ROLE IF NOT EXISTS log_analyzer;
GRANT IMPORTED PRIVILEGES ON DATABASE snowflake TO ROLE log_analyzer;
```

GRANTS_TO_ROLES

This view lists the different privileges granted to Snowflake roles. As mentioned earlier in Chapter 6, "Authorization: Data Access Control," privileges in Snowflake are given strictly to roles, and this view contains all the different privileges that were granted to roles, including those which were revoked. From a security point of view, sometimes the latter tend to be significant, and monitoring the deleted privileges may be as beneficial as looking at the existing privileges. When using this view, keep in mind that it has a latency of up to two hours.

This view contains the following data:

- CREATED_ON, MODIFIED_ON, DELETED_ON – When was the privilege created, modified, and deleted (NULL if not deleted)?

- PRIVILEGE – What type of privilege is this (e.g., ownership, usage, delete, select)?

- GRANTED_ON – The object type on which the privilege was granted (e.g., table, schema, database, file format).

- NAME – The object name on which the privilege is granted (e.g., the table name, schema name, database name, or file format type).

- TABLE_CATALOG, TABLE_SCHEMA – The database and schema in which the object is located.

- GRANTED_TO is always the string "role," probably there to remind us that all privileges in Snowflake are assigned to roles.

- GRANTEE_NAME, GRANTED_BY – The role to which this privilege is granted and the role which granted this privilege.

- GRANT_OPTION – If the value is TRUE, the grantee may grant this privilege to other roles.

Examples

The following query will retrieve the list of 20 last revoked privileges:

```
SELECT * FROM snowflake.account_usage.grants_to_roles
WHERE DELETED_ON IS NOT NULL
ORDER BY DELETED_ON DESC
LIMIT 20;
```

The following query will retrieve the list of 20 last changes/grants to the PUBLIC role. Note that granting privileges to the PUBLIC role is recommended to be used sparingly, as this role is given to all users.

```
SELECT * FROM snowflake.account_usage.grants_to_roles
WHERE DELETED_ON IS NULL
AND GRANTEE_NAME='PUBLIC'
ORDER BY MODIFIED_ON DESC
LIMIT 20;
```

GRANTS_TO_USERS

This view lists the roles which were granted to the users in your Snowflake account, including those which were revoked. When using this view, keep in mind that it has a latency of up to two hours.

This view contains the following data:

- CREATED_ON, DELETED_ON – When was the privilege created and deleted (NULL if not deleted)?

- ROLE – Which role was granted to the user?

- GRANTED_TO is always the string "user".

- GRANTEE_NAME, GRANTED_BY – The user to which this role is granted and the role which granted this role.

Examples

The following query retrieved all users which were granted with the ACCOUNTADMIN role. You'd want to limit this role to a small selection of administrators and enforce the strongest access control and auditing on them, as this is the equivalent of a root access to a server.

```
SELECT * FROM snowflake.account_usage.grants_to_users
WHERE ROLE='ACCOUNTADMIN'
AND DELETED_ON IS NULL;
```

LOGIN_HISTORY

This view is also known in other databases and systems as the access log, and it shows all failed and successful logins to your account. Login events are significant security events and should be audited and monitored both from a security point of view and from a compliance point of view. When using this view, keep in mind that it has a latency of up to two hours.

This view contains the following data:

- EVENT_ID – An identifier for the login event; may be helpful when joining with the SESSIONS view.

- EVENT_TIMESTAMP – The timestamp of the login event.

- EVENT_TYPE is always "LOGIN".

- USER_NAME – The user who made the failed/successful login.

- CLIENT_IP – The IP address from which the user connected.

- REPORTED_CLIENT_TYPE and REPORTED_CLIENT_VERSION – The tool reported by the user when connecting.

- FIRST_AUTHENTICATION_FACTOR – The authentication factor used, such as PASSWORD or OAUTH_ACCESS_TOKEN.

- SECOND_AUTHENTICATION_FACTOR – The second authentication factor used by the user (NULL if none), for example, DUO_PASSCODE.

- IS_SUCCESS – Whether the login attempt was successful.

- ERROR_CODE and ERROR_MESSAGE – The error which prevented the login from being successful.

Examples

The following query shows the top ten users with the most IP addresses used for logins in the last month. Users connecting from several different IP addresses may indicate a security issue or a need to revise the network policies (see the corresponding chapter):

```
SELECT USER_NAME, COUNT(DISTINCT CLIENT_IP) AS NUM_OF_IPS
FROM snowflake.account_usage.login_history
WHERE EVENT_TIMESTAMP >= TIMESTAMPADD(MONTH, -1, CURRENT_TIMESTAMP())
```

```
GROUP BY 1
ORDER BY 2 DESC
LIMIT 10;
```

The following query shows the last ten failed logins in our system (remember that it takes up to two hours for the logins to appear in the view):

```
SELECT EVENT_TIMESTAMP, USER_NAME, CLIENT_IP, REPORTED_CLIENT_TYPE, FIRST_
AUTHENTICATION_FACTOR, SECOND_AUTHENTICATION_FACTOR, ERROR_CODE, ERROR_
MESSAGE
FROM snowflake.account_usage.login_history
WHERE IS_SUCCESS = 'NO'
ORDER BY event_timestamp DESC
LIMIT 10;
```

The following query shows the top ten users with the most failed logins in the last month:

```
SELECT USER_NAME, COUNT(1) AS NUM_OF_FAILED_LOGINS
FROM snowflake.account_usage.login_history
WHERE EVENT_TIMESTAMP >= TIMESTAMPADD(MONTH, -1, CURRENT_TIMESTAMP())
AND IS_SUCCESS='NO'
GROUP BY 1
ORDER BY 2 DESC
LIMIT 10;
```

SESSIONS

This view has a high resemblance to the LOGIN_HISTORY view. It holds information about the successful sessions only, but holds more specific data about the client environment and the client applications used to connect to Snowflake. Since queries have the session identifier in the query log, the data from the sessions view can be easily joined with the data in the QUERY_HISTORY view, to create an enriched audit of queries. The data is populated in latency of up to three hours, so keep in mind that due to the QUERY_HISTORY view's shorter latency (up to 45 minutes), you may get queries which still don't have recorded session information.

Examples

The following query uses this view together with the QUERY_HISTORY, to list SELECT queries done by admin roles using a password authentication in the last month. As we mentioned in the authentication method, administrators retrieving data using password authentication is risky and should be avoided.

```
SELECT START_TIME, QUERY_HISTORY.USER_NAME, ROLE_NAME, ERROR_CODE, ERROR_
MESSAGE, QUERY_TEXT, AUTHENTICATION_METHOD, CLIENT_APPLICATION_ID
FROM snowflake.account_usage.query_history
LEFT JOIN snowflake.account_usage.sessions ON (query_history.session_id =
sessions.session_id)
WHERE ROLE_NAME LIKE '%ADMIN%'
AND QUERY_TYPE = 'SELECT'
AND AUTHENTICATION_METHOD = 'Password'
AND START_TIME >= TIMESTAMPADD(MONTH, -1, CURRENT_TIMESTAMP())
ORDER BY START_TIME DESC;
```

The following query shows queries using the Python connector and a password authentication in the last month. As we learned in Chapter 4, "Authentication: Keeping Strangers Out," it would be best to transform those scripts to be using key-pair authentication, to reduce their risk.

```
SELECT START_TIME, QUERY_HISTORY.USER_NAME, ROLE_NAME, ERROR_CODE, ERROR_
MESSAGE, QUERY_TEXT, AUTHENTICATION_METHOD, CLIENT_APPLICATION_ID
FROM snowflake.account_usage.query_history
LEFT JOIN snowflake.account_usage.sessions ON (query_history.session_id =
sessions.session_id)
WHERE START_TIME >= TIMESTAMPADD(MONTH, -1, CURRENT_TIMESTAMP())
AND ROLE_NAME LIKE '%ADMIN%'
AND CLIENT_APPLICATION_ID LIKE 'Python%'
ORDER BY START_TIME DESC;
```

MASKING_POLICIES

This view contains the masking policies configured in your Snowflake account. This table is useful to keep track of your masking policies. This can be if you automate the process of managing your dynamic masking or to keep control over changes in masking policies. The importance in tracking changes to masking policies is that this configuration changes the level of masking performed over sensitive data retrieved from your Snowflake account, which may lead to sensitive data exposure, and its audit may also be needed as part of compliance requirements. When using this view, keep in mind that it has a latency of up to two hours.

This view contains the following data:

- POLICY_NAME and POLICY_ID – The name and ID of the masking policy

- POLICY_SCHEMA and POLICY_SCHEMA_ID – The name and ID of the schema where the masking policy belongs

- POLICY_CATALOG and POLICY_CATALOG_ID – The name and ID of the database where the masking policy belongs

- POLICY_OWNER – The role which owns this policy

- POLICY_SIGNATURE – The data type of this signature

- POLICY_RETURN_TYPE – The data type returned by the masking function

- POLICY_BODY – The actual masking policy definition

- POLICY_COMMENT – The comment field used in the CREATE command

- CREATED, LAST_ALTERED, DELETED – The timestamps of creation, modification, and (if applicable) deletion of the masking policy

Examples

The following query returns the ten most recent masking policies which were deleted in our Snowflake account:

```
SELECT POLICY_ID, POLICY_NAME, POLICY_BODY
FROM snowflake.account_usage.masking_policies
WHERE deleted IS NOT NULL
ORDER BY deleted DESC
LIMIT 10;
```

POLICY_REFERENCES

This view shows the columns on which the masking policies are assigned. As you probably remember (and if you don't, feel free to hop to Chapter 6, "Authorization: Data Access Control"), the good thing about dynamic masking is that you're able to set a policy once and then apply it to many different columns. The benefit of monitoring this view is, as mentioned earlier regarding the MASKING_POLICIES view, that changes to masking configuration are changes to the access of sensitive data in your Snowflake account, and as such, changes to it may be risky.

Note that unlike other views in account_usage, here you will not see dropped objects, and likewise, you will not be able to know when masking policies were applied on specific columns. This makes tracking of masking policy assignment (and unassignment) more challenging but not impossible, as you will still be able to see these changes in the QUERY_HISTORY view.

This view contains the following data:

- POLICY_NAME and POLICY_ID – The name and ID of the masking policy assigned

- POLICY_KIND – The type of policy, which is always MASKING_POLICY, to remind us what type of business we're into :)

- REF_DATABASE_NAME and REF_SCHEMA_NAME – The location (database and schema) of the table or view on which the policy is assigned

- REF_ENTITY_NAME – The name of the table or view on which the policy is assigned

- REF_ENTITY_DOMAIN – The type of object (TABLE or VIEW) on which the policy is assigned

- REF_COLUMN_NAME – The specific column on which the policy is assigned

- REF_ARG_COLUMN_NAMES

Examples

The following query shows the dynamic policies assigned in the "production" database:

```
SELECT POLICY_NAME, CONCAT(REF_SCHEMA_NAME, '.', REF_ENTITY_NAME, '.',
REF_COLUMN_NAME)
FROM snowflake.account_usage.policy_references
WHERE REF_DATABASE_NAME='production';
```

QUERY_HISTORY

This is one of the most important metadata views, as it contains all the queries executed on your Snowflake account, in other databases also known as the native audit log or query log. As almost all activities in Snowflake, even those done in the user interface, are done using SQL statements, this will not only show you access to data but also changes to configuration. Note that the data in this view has a latency of up to 45 minutes.

This importance is magnified, as in many other database solutions, you will need to manually set up query logs, which may have an impact on your performance and/or costs, in addition to being an overhead to set up. Having a query log up and running, starting from your first query on Snowflake, and kept for a respectable one-year period, including the out-of-the-box ability to run queries natively on this log, is a major win for Snowflake and its users. In certain cases, you may still want to set up a process that replicates the data to a different location, perhaps even within Snowflake, as directly querying this view is good for ad hoc queries, but for more intense analytics, it can be quite slow.

If that's not cool enough, the QUERY_HISTORY view also contains failed queries, which are sometimes needed to be collected from a separate error log in other databases, and having everything in one place is a blessing in terms of visibility.

This view will be useful in many ways, as it contains a lot of information of different types. Many columns are useful when tracking the performance of your Snowflake account(s), which is outside the scope of this book but may very well be within the scope of your job role, or cool things you can add a lot of value in.

These are the most important columns in this view security-wise:

- QUERY_ID – The unique identifier of the query logged.

- QUERY_TEXT – The actual query sent. Note that although some values are redacted in the query, such as passwords, a lot of data is not redacted. This means that queries may contain sensitive data such as operational or personal information. For example, a query

119

such as INSERT INTO USERS (...) may contain sensitive fields. As a result of that, make sure that you limit access to the QUERY_HISTORY only to a restricted set of users, and if you replicate the table for analytics, make sure you are restrictive about its results as well.

- DATABASE_ID, DATABASE_NAME, SCHEMA_ID, SCHEMA_NAME – The location context when executing the query. Note that even a query running in a context of a specific schema or database can access objects in other databases and schemas by referencing them with their complete path (i.e., database.schema.table or database. schema.view). That means that if you're looking for all queries running against objects in a specific database or schema, you will need to also parse the QUERY_TEXT.

- QUERY_TYPE – The type of query logged, such as SELECT, CREATE, and DROP, but also more specific types such as ALTER_TABLE_ MODIFY_COLUMN which can help you generate specific reports or monitor specific operations.

- SESSION_ID – The session through which this query was executed. This identifier can be used to track all queries sent throughout a specific session, as well as when joined with the SESSIONS view.

- USER_ID – The user who sent the query.

- ROLE_NAME – The role which was used for the query.

- QUERY_TAG – The query tag, which is inherited from the Session.

- EXECUTION_STATUS – The status of the query, which can be SUCCESS, FAIL, or INCIDENT.

- ERROR_CODE and ERROR_MESSAGE – The error which prevented the query from being successful.

- START_TIME and END_TIME – The start and end timestamps of the query execution.

Note that we've omitted many columns which contain interesting information (such as credits used, execution time, and more). For the complete listing of columns, visit the relevant Snowflake documentation page.

Examples

The following query shows the latest failed queries which were sent by admin roles:

```
SELECT START_TIME, USER_NAME, ROLE_NAME, ERROR_CODE, ERROR_MESSAGE, QUERY_
TYPE, QUERY_TEXT FROM snowflake.account_usage.query_history
WHERE ROLE_NAME LIKE '%ADMIN%'
AND EXECUTION_STATUS = 'FAIL'
ORDER BY START_TIME DESC
LIMIT 50;
```

The following query shows the users with the most query errors in the last month (which may or may not be due to suspicious behavior, you will probably need to also tune this according to specific error types):

```
SELECT USER_NAME, COUNT(*) AS num_of_errors FROM snowflake.account_usage.
query_history
WHERE EXECUTION_STATUS = 'FAIL'
GROUP BY USER_NAME
ORDER BY num_of_errors DESC
LIMIT 10;
```

The following query lists all SELECT queries done on the database accounting by using any admin role (as we mentioned earlier in Chapter 6, "Authorization: Data Access Control," using admin roles to query data is a bad security practice):

```
SELECT START_TIME, USER_NAME, ROLE_NAME, ERROR_CODE, ERROR_MESSAGE, QUERY_
TYPE, QUERY_TEXT FROM snowflake.account_usage.query_history
WHERE ROLE_NAME LIKE '%ADMIN%'
AND QUERY_TYPE = 'SELECT'
AND START_TIME >= TIMESTAMPADD(MONTH, -1, CURRENT_TIMESTAMP())
AND DATABASE_NAME = 'accounting'
ORDER BY START_TIME DESC;
```

ROLES

This view shows you a list of the roles configured in your Snowflake account. This is a fairly simple view, with the role name, timestamps of its creation and deletion (if it was deleted), and comments (if such were added to the role).

121

Examples

Use the following query to show all the roles added throughout the last month:

```
SELECT NAME, CREATED_ON FROM snowflake.account_usage.roles
WHERE CREATED_ON >= TIMESTAMPADD(MONTH, -1, CURRENT_TIMESTAMP())
ORDER BY CREATED_ON DESC;
```

STAGES

The stages view lists the stages configured in your Snowflake account, as well as those which were deleted. If you'd like to refresh your knowledge about stages and how they're used, you can read the documentation or revisit Chapter 3, "Data Encryption and Ingestion." However, depending on the organization, it may very well be that various teams have, over the months or years, uploaded files to staging, which contains sensitive information, and just remained there.

This, in terms of security, can be very bad, the equivalent of forgetting files in public cloud storage buckets. Oh, wait a minute, they ARE in public cloud storage buckets. In all seriousness though, that CSV file which contained personal information of ACME Candies' customers or employees, and was used just temporarily, after which its tables were created...? We'd better make sure that its stage files were also removed.

Another security risk is a stage which was uploaded and owned by a widely used role (such as PUBLIC, of course). There is no contradiction between this and the previous risk. Someone might have used the PUBLIC role to create a stage and import data, and the data wasn't deleted and is now accessible by a lot of users.

Once you find these stages (see the following examples for the query, or simply use SHOW STAGES or SHOW STAGES LIKE for a quick listing), you may want to check what they contain. To do that, you can use the LIST command (LIST @<stage name>) and then the following command to directly explore the data in those files:

```
// lists the 2 first columns from the file
SELECT $1, $2 FROM @<stage name>/<path>;
```

For more information about working with stages, please refer to the documentation. These are the columns in this view:

- STAGE_ID and STAGE_NAME – The identifier and name of the stage.

- STAGE_CATALOG_ID, STAGE_CATALOG, STAGE_SCHEMA_ID, and STAGE_SCHEMA – The database and schema associated with the stage.

- STAGE_URL – The URL of the stage (if it's an external stage), such as the s3 bucket URL.

- STAGE_REGION – The region where the stage is located (e.g., us-east-1).

- STAGE_TYPE – The type of stage, Internal Named, External Named, User, or Table. For more information about the differences, refer to the Snowflake documentation, but the most important one in terms of the security risk scenario mentioned before is the External Named stage type.

- STAGE_OWNER – The role that owns the stage (unless it was deleted).

- CREATED, LAST_ALTERED, DELETED – The timestamps of creation, modification, and (if applicable) deletion of the stage.

Examples

The following query retrieves a list of all currently active stages (of all types), owned by the PUBLIC role (meaning they're open to all Snowflake users):

```
SELECT STAGE_NAME, STAGE_CATALOG, STAGE_SCHEMA, STAGE_TYPE, STAGE_URL,
CREATED
FROM snowflake.account_usage.stages
WHERE STAGE_OWNER = 'PUBLIC'
AND DELETED IS NULL
ORDER BY CREATED;
```

The following query retrieves the ten oldest external stages which are still active:

```
SELECT STAGE_NAME, STAGE_CATALOG, STAGE_SCHEMA, STAGE_TYPE, STAGE_URL,
CREATED
FROM snowflake.account_usage.stages
WHERE STAGE_TYPE = 'External Named'
AND DELETED IS NULL
ORDER BY CREATED
LIMIT 10;
```

TASK_HISTORY

The task history view shows details about the execution of Snowflake tasks. Note that the queries running as tasks are also present in the QUERY_HISTORY view, so auditing the TASK_HISTORY view does not fix any blind spots. The main security benefit is if you have a specific issue you want to investigate around task execution. The latency for this view is up to 45 minutes, and the retention time is 1 year.

The view contains the following columns:

- QUERY_ID – The query ID, which you can use to join the data with the QUERY_HISTORY view, in case you need additional information from there

- NAME – The name of the task

- DATABASE_NAME and SCHEMA_NAME – The location of this task

- QUERY_TEXT – The actual query that the task runs

- CONDITION_TEXT – The WHEN condition that determines whether the task should run

- STATE – The completion state of this task, which can be SUCCEEDED, FAILED, CANCELLED, or SKIPPED

- ERROR_CODE and ERROR_MESSAGES – The error returned by the query execution of the task (if there was one)

- SCHEDULED_TIME, QUERY_START_TIME, COMPLETED_ON – The timestamp in which this task was scheduled, started, and completed

- ROOT_TASK_ID – The root task in the task hierarchy which started the trigger flow leading to this task

- GRAPH_VERSION – The version of the task tree, where each increment means a modification to one of the tasks. This helps you understand what happened before and after changes to the task tree.

- RUN_ID – The start time (epoch) of the run of the task tree

- RETURN_VALUE – The returned value that the task returns to its child tasks (if relevant)

Examples

The following query lists the last ten tasks which were executed with an
ACCOUNTADMIN role (which should not be used for task execution):

```
SELECT name, task_history.database_name, task_history.schema_name, query_
history.query_text, condition_text
FROM snowflake.account_usage.task_history
LEFT JOIN snowflake.account_usage.query_history ON (task_history.query_id =
query_history.query_id)
WHERE role_name LIKE '%ADMIN%'
ORDER BY scheduled_time DESC
LIMIT 10;
```

USERS

The USERS view shows a listing of the users in the account. This includes users which
were deleted (up to the retention period of one year) and is useful for monitoring
users with lacking authentication configuration (for more information on that, revisit
Chapter 4, "Authentication: Keeping Strangers Out"). You can also monitor users who
are not in use, in which case it may be a good idea to suspend or terminate the users, as
having such stale users who are not really using the system is usually a risk without any
value. The data latency for this view is up to two hours.

If you are looking for an up-to-date listing of your users, you can use the SHOW
USERS command instead.

The view contains the following columns:

- NAME and LOGIN_NAME – The user's unique identifier name and
  login name, which will in most cases be the same (except lowercase
  vs. uppercase). They can be different values, but each needs to be
  unique.

- DISPLAY_NAME – The display name, which does not have to be
  unique.

- CREATED_ON – The timestamp of creation for the user.

- DELETED_ON – The timestamp of deletion (in case the user was
  deleted).

- FIRST_NAME and LAST_NAME – The user's name, in case it was set.

- EMAIL – The user's email address.

- MUST_CHANGE_PASSWORD – If set to true, the user will be forced to change their password on the next login attempt. As mentioned in Chapter 4, "Authentication: Keeping Strangers Out," it is highly recommended to set this to true when setting up new accounts.

- HAS_PASSWORD – Specifies whether the user has a password configured.

- COMMENT – A comment field.

- DISABLED – Specifies whether the user is disabled (prevented from logging in).

- SNOWFLAKE_LOCK – Specifies whether the user is temporarily locked (for multiple failed login attempts).

- LOCKED_UNTIL_TIME – Specifies the number of minutes left until the user is unlocked (if it is temporarily locked).

- DEFAULT_WAREHOUSE – The warehouse used by the user, unless another is specified in the connection string, or changed with the USE WAREHOUSE command.

- DEFAULT_NAMESPACE – The default namespace (database or database and schema) in which the user is, unless otherwise specified in the connection string or changed with the USE command.

- DEFAULT_ROLE – The default role to be used by the user, unless otherwise specified in the connection string or changed with the USE ROLE command. To prevent admin role abuse, it is a best practice to never have the default role as an administrative role.

- EXT_AUTHN_DUO and EXT_AUTHN_UID – Whether the Duo MFA is active, and the ID of the authorization ID used by the Duo MFA. For more information about the Duo MFA, refer to Chapter 4, "Authentication: Keeping Strangers Out."

- BYPASS_MFA_UNTIL – In case there is a temporary bypass of MFA set for the user, this will show you until when it's bypassed.

- LAST_SUCCESS_LOGIN – The timestamp of the latest successful login, which can be helpful when looking for stale users.

- EXPIRES_AT – An automated expiration timestamp for the user. This can be useful for setting up a temporary user.

- HAS_RSA_PUBLIC_KEY – Specifies whether the user has a key pair configured in this Snowflake account. For more information about authentication using key pair, refer to Chapter 4, "Authentication: Keeping Strangers Out."

Examples

The following query shows all user accounts starting with "SVC" or "APP" that do not have a key-pair authentication set up or have a password authentication set up. As per Chapter 4, "Authentication: Keeping Strangers Out," it is recommended to use key-pair authentication for nonhuman users.

```
SELECT name, email, created_on
FROM snowflake.account_usage.users
WHERE (name ILIKE 'SVC%' OR name ILIKE 'APP%')
AND HAS_RSA_PUBLIC_KEY = FALSE
AND HAS_PASSWORD = TRUE;
```

The following query shows all active users (not deleted or disabled) that haven't logged in in the last three months. It is recommended to disable stale users.

```
SELECT name, email, created_on
FROM snowflake.account_usage.users
WHERE disabled = FALSE
AND deleted_on IS NULL
AND last_success_login <= TIMESTAMPADD(MONTH, -3, CURRENT_TIMESTAMP());
```

The following query shows all users with a default role set to an administrative role:

```
SELECT name, email, created_on
FROM snowflake.account_usage.users
WHERE default_role LIKE '%ADMIN%';
```

127

ACCESS_HISTORY

ACCESS_HISTORY is a view which is still in public preview at the time of writing and is only open to enterprise accounts. This view contains detailed information about the locations which were accessed by each query. This view can be useful when joined with the QUERY_HISTORY table, to get specific details about which data was accessed in each query or to create reports or investigate access to specific locations. The data latency of this view is three hours, and the data is retained for one year (note that QUERY_HISTORY has a shorter data latency time of 45 minutes, so expect differences in recent data between the two views).

Note that this view only contains SELECT operations (even if internal), but not other operations like UPDATE, INSERT, MERGE, etc.

The view contains the following columns:

- QUERY_ID – The query ID, which can be used for joining with the QUERY_HISTORY view.

- QUERY_START_TIME – The start time of the query.

- USER_NAME – The username of the user who ran the query.

- DIRECT_OBJECTS_ACCESSED – This is a JSON object, containing an array with all the columns accessed by the query, per table or view being accessed.

- BASE_OBJECTS_ACCESSED – This is a JSON object, containing an array with all the underlying columns accessed by the query (always down to the table level, no views).

Examples

The following query returns all users who accessed any cc_num column in any table of the current ACME Candies' account, with the number of times they've accessed it:

```
SELECT USER_NAME, COUNT(*)
FROM snowflake.account_usage.access_history,
lateral flatten(base_objects_accessed) root,
lateral flatten(root.value) tbls,
lateral flatten(tbls.value) clmns
```

```
WHERE clmns.value:"columnName" = 'CC_NUM'
GROUP BY 1
ORDER BY 2;
```

7.2.3. The Reader Accounts Schema

The READER_ACCOUNT schema in the SNOWFLAKE database lists the metadata views specific for reader accounts. As they are a modified subset of the ACCOUNT_USAGE schema, we will list the relevant views, along with the relevant columns, but we will not list the complete columns listing, as this can be found earlier, in the ACCOUNT_USAGE schema (or you may refer to the Snowflake documentation).

The two relevant views for reader accounts auditing and monitoring are LOGIN_ HISTORY, listing the access attempts (successful and unsuccessful), and QUERY_ HISTORY, listing the queries being run by reader accounts.

In the login history view, you will see the additional field READER_ACCOUNT_ NAME, with the name of the reader account connecting to the Snowflake account to retrieve data. The same column also exists in the READER_ACCOUNT.QUERY_HISTORY view, which also has several columns missing, none of which were discussed before as part of the columns interesting for security reasons.

To learn more about reader accounts, refer to Chapter 8, "Secure Data Sharing with Snowflake."

7.2.4. Views in the Information Schema

Each database in Snowflake has a schema called INFORMATION_SCHEMA, which holds metadata specific to that database. In the beginning of this section, we discussed the differences between this schema and the SNOWFLAKE.ACCOUNT_USAGE schema, but as a reminder, the views in INFORMATION_SCHEMA are more fresh (has no latency when data is inserted), but historical events are retained for shorter periods. In several cases, it doesn't matter which database's INFORMATION_SCHEMA you're querying; you will get the same results (this is for account-level settings).

Here are the relevant views to security in INFORMATION_SCHEMA.

APPLICABLE_ROLES

This view shows a list of roles granted either to other roles or to users. Note that you will only be able to retrieve grants which are granted to your current user or to one of the roles available to your user. Depending on the use case, you can use this view instead of GRANTS_TO_USERS or GRANTS_TO_ROLES, to find out to whom a role is granted. The advantage is that you will get completely up-to-date information, and the disadvantages are that you will not see past grants (revoked grants) and that you will get the grantee in one column, whether it's a user or a role, and with no indicator of which type it is.

The view contains the following columns:

- ROLE_NAME – The role that is granted.

- GRANTEE – The role or user to which the role is granted.

- ROLE_OWNER – The role owning the role that is granted.

- IS_GRANTABLE – Is this role self-granted (can someone with this role grant it to others)?

Examples

The following query checks the role granted to the current user or the current role (can be used for access control filters, or as part of administrative applications):

```
SELECT role_name
FROM information_schema.applicable_roles
WHERE grantee = CURRENT_USER()
OR grantee = CURRENT_ROLE()
ORDER BY role_name;
```

ENABLED_ROLES

This view contains only the roles enabled for the current specific role (in addition to the PUBLIC role, which is enabled for all roles). Since this runs in the context of the current role executing the query, you will only get partial information about the roles which you can use with the current user, and as such (and in light of more informative views), this view is less informative than others about the same data you may want to retrieve.

The view contains only two columns – the ROLE_NAME and ROLE_OWNER, both of the granted roles.

OBJECT_PRIVILEGES

This view contains the privileges granted on different objects for your currently used role. Since this view is quick and up to date, it can be used for administrative purposes (e.g., if you want to create a role management overlay on top of Snowflake). An important thing to note is that this view is specific to each database, and so, if you choose to retrieve it, you may want to retrieve it from certain databases or from all of them.

The view contains the following columns:

- GRANTOR – The role who granted the object.

- GRANTEE – The role who was granted with the object.

- OBJECT_CATALOG and OBJECT_SCHEMA – The database and schema in which the object is located.

- OBJECT_NAME – The object for which the privilege was granted.

- OBJECT_TYPE – The type of object (e.g., TABLE, VIEW, USER, ROLE, etc.).

- PRIVILEGE_TYPE – The type of action granted in this privilege.

- IS_GRANTABLE – Whether the grantee can grant this privilege to other roles.

- CREATED – The timestamp in which this privilege was granted. As a reminder, this is a configuration view and does not list revoked privileges.

Examples

The following query retrieves the list of all the functions in the database which are granted to the current role used in the query:

```
SELECT grantor, grantee, object_catalog, object_schema, object_name,
privilege_type, is_grantable, created
FROM information_schema.object_privileges
WHERE OBJECT_TYPE='FUNCTION';
```

STAGES

The importance of monitoring stages was mentioned earlier when discussing the SNOWFLAKE.ACCOUNT_USAGE.STAGES view. Since this view is relevant for the current role of the user, it is less useful than the one in ACCOUNT_USAGE for housekeeping purposes across your account, but since it's updated in real time, it can be more useful in the administering stage useful if you're creating an in-house management overlay. Also keep in mind that this view is specific for the current database queried, so if you want to query all stages available for your role, you will need to iterate through all available databases.

The view contains the following columns:

- STAGE_CATALOG and STAGE_SCHEMA – The database and schema where this stage is configured.

- STAGE_NAME – The name of the stage.

- STAGE_URL – The location of the stage (e.g., s3://acme_candies_ ingestion).

- STAGE_REGION – The region of the stage.

- STAGE_TYPE – The type of stage, Internal Named, External Named, User, or Table. For more information about the differences, refer to the Snowflake documentation, but the most important one in terms of the security risk scenario mentioned previously is the External Named stage type.

- STAGE_OWNER – The role owning this stage.

- COMMENT – The comment added using the CREATE STAGE command.

- CREATED and LAST_ALTERED – The timestamps of creation and last change of this stage.

Examples

The following query retrieves a list of all external stages in the current database:

```
SELECT stage_name, stage_url, stage_region, stage_owner, created,
last_altered
FROM information_schema.stages
WHERE stage_type='External Named';
```

TABLE_PRIVILEGES

This view contains the configuration of privileges in the current database for tables. The results are a subset of the OBJECT_PRIVILEGES (if you filter by `object_type = 'TABLE'`). As with other database-level information schema views, if you require data for multiple databases, you will need to iterate through them, and the data you're getting is limited to the current running role. On the other hand, the data in this view is immediately updated as changes are made, unlike the SNOWFLAKE.ACCOUNT_USAGE.GRANTS_TO_ROLES view, so it can be used when you require up-to-date configuration information.

The view contains the following columns:

- GRANTOR – The role that granted the privilege.

- GRANTEE – The role that was granted with the privilege.

- TABLE_CATALOG and TABLE_SCHEMA – The location (database and schema) of the table.

- TABLE_NAME – The name of the table.

- PRIVILEGE_TYPE – The type of privilege (e.g., SELECT, UPDATE, INSERT). Note that if the user has ownership of the table, it will not list the implicit underlying permissible actions.

- IS_GRANTABLE – Whether the grantee can further grant this privilege.

- CREATED – The timestamp of creation of the table.

Examples

The following query retrieves a list of tables which are regrantable, in case we want to make some limitations over these in ACME Candies:

```
SELECT grantor, grantee, table_catalog, table_schema, table_name,
privilege_type
FROM information_schema.table_privileges
WHERE is_grantable='YES';
```

Other Views

In addition to the security views listed earlier, in the documentation, you can find a full list of the views. Some of these can help you get lists of all objects in Snowflake (such as tables, views, functions, external tables, and more). You can definitely use such tables in good ways, such as to help you prepare a data inventory that will help you to better control the data you have in your Snowflake account. You can also make a lot of operational value from analyzing the data in the metadata to learn more about actions which can impact your performance and costs.

7.2.5. Table Functions in the Information Schema

In addition to metadata coming from views, there is also metadata that can be pulled by using specific table functions. These functions accept certain parameters and then return the result as a table.

Access to these table functions is available to ACCOUNTADMIN and may also be granted by granting the MONITOR USAGE global privilege. ACCOUNTADMIN should not be used for "everyday monitoring" and should be granted from this role to another administrative role with lesser privileges, so we don't expose all the ACCOUNTADMIN privileges for the users who are allowed to monitor our Snowflake.

In ACME Candies, the chosen role is log_analyzer, and so, as an ACCOUNTADMIN, let's create the new role and grant it with the required privileges:

```
CREATE ROLE IF NOT EXISTS log_analyzer;
GRANT MONITOR USAGE ON ACCOUNT TO ROLE log_analyzer;
```

In the following are some of the more useful table functions in terms of security value.

EXTERNAL_FUNCTIONS_HISTORY

This table function can be used to pull information about the external functions which were triggered by your queries. The significance is that such external functions are receiving data from your SQL queries, and as they're external to Snowflake, data is leaving your Snowflake account, and so it's important to monitor this behavior. There is a retention time limit of six months over this information.

Since the data is aggregated and will not show you information such as the users or roles using those functions, it is useful for noticing anomalies, but in order to investigate these, you will need to query the logs in SNOWFLAKE.ACCOUNT_USAGE.QUERY_HISTORY.

The function accepts the following arguments:

- DATE_RANGE_START – Optionally providing the beginning of the time range to query. If not provided, it's defaulted to ten minutes prior to DATE_RANGE_END.

- DATE_RANGE_END – Optionally providing the end of the time range to query. If not provided, it's defaulted to CURRENT_DATE.

- FUNCTION_SIGNATURE – Optionally providing a specific external function's signature to query for. The signature is the full location of the function, with the argument types, for example, eu_candies.research.enrich_flavors(integer, integer).

Notes:

1. Unfortunately, although you're not required to provide the FUNCTION_SIGNATURE, failure to do so will result in very partial information, which lacks most of the returned fields.

2. The results are returned aggregated per period of time. The period of these "buckets" is determined by the range of time requested.

The function returns the following columns:

- START_TIME and END_TIME – The time range of the bucket described in this row

- NAME – The name of the external function

- ARGUMENTS – The data types of the arguments and of the return value (e.g., `GET_CANDY_FLAVORS(INTEGER) RETURN VARCHAR`)

- FUNCTION_ENDPOINT_URL – The HTTPS API endpoint

- SOURCE_CLOUD, SOURCE_REGION – The source cloud and region from which the data was sent

- TARGET_CLOUD, TARGET_REGION – The target cloud and regions to which the data was sent

- INVOCATIONS – The number of API calls performed in the time range

- SENT_ROWS – The number of rows sent to the API endpoint in the time range

- RECEIVED_ROWS – The number of rows returned by the API endpoint in the time range

- SENT_BYTES – The number of bytes sent to the API endpoint in the time range

- RECEIVED_BYTES – The number of bytes returned by the API endpoint in the time range

Examples

The following query retrieves external function metrics about functions running in the last six months, in one-day buckets (note that since the data is aggregated, you will not get a breakdown of the actual functions):

```
SELECT start_time, end_time, invocations, sent_rows, received_rows, sent_
bytes, received_bytes
FROM TABLE(information_schema.external_functions_history(
    date_range_start => DATEADD('day', -180, CURRENT_TIMESTAMP())));
```

The following query retrieves the specific data about the ENRICH_QUERY external function:

```
SELECT *
FROM TABLE(information_schema.external_functions_history(
    date_range_start => DATEADD('day', -180, CURRENT_TIMESTAMP()),
    function_signature => 'acme_candies.research.enrich_flavor(integer)'));
```

LOGIN_HISTORY

This function returns the same fields that are returned by the SNOWFLAKE.ACCOUNT_
USAGE.LOGIN_HISTORY view. Its main advantage over the account usage view is
that it has no data latency, and so it will return even the most recent logins. Its main
disadvantage is the retention period – you can return only information about logins
performed in the last seven days (unlike one year in the account usage view).

This function returns only the results per your current role's privilege. That means
that you will only get the results for the users owned by you. For a "regular" user, this will
be yourself, but if your current role owns users, you will see their logins as well.

The function accepts the following arguments:

- TIME_RANGE_START – Optionally providing the beginning of
  the time range to query. Note that since this request returns only
  a limited amount of results, they will be determined by the TIME_
  RANGE_END. That means that if you choose a TIME_RANGE_
  START of seven days ago and a TIME_RANGE_END of CURRENT_
  TIMESTAMP, the oldest event returned will be TIME_RANGE_END
  minus RESULT_LIMIT events.

- TIME_RANGE_END – Optionally providing the end of the time range
  to query. If not provided, it's defaulted to the most recent event.

- RESULT_LIMIT – The number of results to return, up to 10,000
  (default is 100).

The function returns the same columns as the LOGIN_HISTORY view:

- EVENT_ID – An identifier for the login event may be helpful when
  joining with the SESSIONS view.

- EVENT_TIMESTAMP – The timestamp of the login event.

- EVENT_TYPE is always "LOGIN".

- USER_NAME – The user who made the failed/successful login.

- CLIENT_IP – The IP address from which the user connected.

- REPORTED_CLIENT_TYPE and REPORTED_CLIENT_VERSION –
  The tool reported by the user when connecting.

- FIRST_AUTHENTICATION_FACTOR – The authentication factor used, such as PASSWORD or OAUTH_ACCESS_TOKEN.

- SECOND_AUTHENTICATION_FACTOR – The second authentication factor used by the user (NULL if none), for example, DUO_PASSCODE.

- IS_SUCCESS – Whether the login attempt was successful.

- ERROR_CODE and ERROR_MESSAGE – The error which prevented the login from being successful.

Examples

The following query shows the last ten unsuccessful login attempts (within the last 10,000 results, which is the maximum amount of results to check):

```
SELECT *
FROM TABLE(information_schema.login_history(
    result_limit => 10000))
WHERE is_success='NO'
LIMIT 10;
```

LOGIN_HISTORY_BY_USER

This function is identical to the LOGIN_HISTORY function described earlier, with the only change being that it also accepts a user argument, which it filters by. This makes it a better option to use, obviously, when you're looking into logins of specific users.

The added argument, USER_NAME, is defaulted to the current user, if this argument is not provided. The function returns the same columns as LOGIN_HISTORY.

Examples

The following query shows all logins (assuming they're under 100) performed by the user Ben, between five and six days ago:

```
SELECT *
FROM TABLE(information_schema.login_history_by_user(
    user_name => 'BEN',
    time_range_start => dateadd('day',-6,current_timestamp()),
    time_range_end => dateadd('day',-5,current_timestamp())
));
```

POLICY_REFERENCES

This function gets information similar to the one returned by the account usage view POLICY_REFERENCES and requires the ACCOUNTADMIN role to be executed. The Account Usage view is more useful, as it can also be used by other roles as well, while the advantage of this function is that it has no data latency. In most cases, this will matter less, and thus, it is advised to use the account usage view.

QUERY_HISTORY

This function returns data from the query log and will return the same columns as SNOWFLAKE.ACCOUNT_USAGE.QUERY_HISTORY will. There are a few differences between the view and the function:

1. Access to this function is available to all roles. It will show you the query history for your use, and if you have the MONITOR privilege, you will also be able to see other users' queries.

2. You will get queries without any data latency. In fact, if you query for the newest queries, you will even get the query you used against this function within the results.

3. Results are limited for seven days (as opposed to one year in the account usage view).

The function accepts the following arguments:

- END_TIME_RANGE_START – Yes, this may sound a bit confusing, but since the function is retrieving results by the query's end time, this indicates the earliest query end_time to be returned.

- END_TIME_RANGE_END – This parameter indicates the latest end_time in the time range.

- RESULT_LIMIT – The limit of results to be returned (up to 10,000, default is 100).

The function returns the same columns as the LOGIN_HISTORY view. Since there are a large number of columns returned, here are the most important ones in terms of security (you can find the full listing in the documentation):

- QUERY_ID – The unique identifier of the query logged.

- QUERY_TEXT – The actual query sent. Note that although some values are redacted in the query, such as passwords, a lot of data is not redacted. This means that queries may contain sensitive data such as operational or personal information. For example, a query such as INSERT INTO USERS (...) may contain sensitive fields. As a result of that, make sure that you limit access to the QUERY_HISTORY only to a restricted set of users, and if you replicate the table for analytics, make sure you are restrictive about its results as well.

- DATABASE_ID, DATABASE_NAME, SCHEMA_ID, SCHEMA_NAME – The location context when executing the query. Note that even a query running in a context of a specific schema or database can access objects in other databases and schemas by referencing them with their complete path (i.e., database.schema.table or database.schema.view). That means that if you're looking for all queries running against objects in a specific database or schema, you will need to also parse the QUERY_TEXT.

- QUERY_TYPE – The type of query logged, such as SELECT, CREATE, and DROP, but also more specific types such as ALTER_TABLE_MODIFY_COLUMN which can help you generate specific reports or monitor specific operations.

- SESSION_ID – The session through which this query was executed. This identifier can be used to track all queries sent throughout a specific session, as well as when joined with the SESSIONS view.

- USER_ID – The user who sent the query.

- ROLE_NAME – The role which was used for the query.

- QUERY_TAG – The query tag, which is inherited from the Session.

- EXECUTION_STATUS – The status of the query, which can be SUCCESS, FAIL, or INCIDENT.

- ERROR_CODE and ERROR_MESSAGE – The error which prevented the query from being successful.

- START_TIME and END_TIME – The start and end timestamps of the query execution.

Examples

The following query retrieves the last ten queries, excluding the query used to retrieve the query history. If you have the MONITOR privilege in the role used for this query, it will be across all users:

```
SELECT *
FROM TABLE(information_schema.query_history(result_limit => 11))
LIMIT 10 OFFSET 1;
```

QUERY_HISTORY_BY_*

If you want to filter by additional dimensions, there are currently three specific functions which enable you to do so:

- QUERY_HISTORY_BY_SESSION – This function behaves the same as QUERY_HISTORY, but accepts an additional parameter, session_id, which accepts either a session ID or CURRENT_SESSION.

- QUERY_HISTORY_BY_USER – This function behaves the same as QUERY_HISTORY, but accepts an additional parameter, user_name, which can either be the username or CURRENT_USER (which is the default).

- QUERY_HISTORY_BY_WAREHOUSE – This function behaves the same as QUERY_HISTORY, but accepts an additional parameter, warehouse_name, which accepts either a warehouse name or CURRENT_WAREHOUSE (which is the default).

REST_EVENT_HISTORY

This function returns the log information from the SCIM API calls made to your Snowflake account. If you recall, SCIM is used in user provisioning integration, as we've seen in Chapter 4, "Authentication: Keeping Strangers Out." The function can help you debug issues during provisioning setup or problems, but since SCIM is a very powerful tool, it should also be used to monitor SCIM activity and to make sure that this is not used in a careless or malicious way.

Keep in mind that the retention period is seven days, and so, it would make sense to make a task that pulls the log into a more long-term repository. This function requires an ACCOUNTADMIN role to be executed, and unfortunately, the privilege can't be granted to other roles.

The function accepts the following arguments:

- REST_SERVICE_TYPE – This is a required parameter and should always be SCIM.

- TIME_RANGE_START – The timestamp to return events later than. If this parameter is not provided, it will default to seven days ago.

- TIME_RANGE_START – The timestamp to return events later than. If this parameter is not provided, it will default to CURRENT_TIMESTAMP.

- RESULT_LIMIT – The limit of results to be returned (up to 10,000, default is 100).

The function returns the following columns:

- EVENT_TIMESTAMP – The timestamp of the API call.

- EVENT_ID – The event identifier.

- EVENT_TYPE – This will always be SCIM (as it's the only supported rest API at the moment).

- ENDPOINT – The API endpoint relative URL.

- METHOD – The HTTP method used.

- STATUS – The HTTP status of the result.

- ERROR_CODE – The error code (if there was an error).

- DETAILS – JSON description of the result of the API call.

- CLIENT_IP – The client IP used to make the API CALL.

- ACTOR_NAME – The name of the actor making the API call.

- ACTOR_DOMAIN – The domain in which the request was made.

- RESOURCE_NAME – The name of the object making the request.

- RESOURCE_DOMAIN – The object type making the request.

Examples

The following query retrieves a list of the failed SCIM API calls. This can be useful in terms of operational issues but can also point to security issues:

```
SELECT *
  FROM TABLE(information_schema.rest_event_history(
      rest_service_type => 'scim',
      result_limit => 10000))
  WHERE ERROR_CODE IS NOT NULL
  ORDER BY event_timestamp DESC;
```

The following query retrieves an aggregation of the IP addresses used for SCIM API calls. As mentioned in Chapter 4, "Authentication: Keeping Strangers Out," it is recommended to apply a network policy on SCIM, and it's advised to make sure only relevant IP addresses are accessing SCIM.

```
SELECT client_ip, COUNT(*)
  FROM TABLE(information_schema.rest_event_history(
      rest_service_type => 'scim',
      result_limit => 10000))
      GROUP BY client_ip
  ORDER BY client_ip DESC;
```

Other Table Functions

In addition to the table functions mentioned earlier, there are more table functions which may be relevant to investigating specific incidents (e.g., when did loading of data happen for a specific table, and from where), and for a full list of the table functions, you can always refer to the Snowflake documentation.

7.2.6. Use Cases

So far throughout this chapter, we've quite extensively given examples of the relevant sources of metadata for Snowflake, on things you can and should monitor and audit in Snowflake. We'd like to now focus on some of the important use cases you'd like to monitor and connect the use cases with some of the locations we mentioned.

Database Access Monitoring

Back in Chapter 4, "Authentication: Keeping Strangers Out," we mentioned how important it is to make sure that whoever "walks" into your data warehouse is authenticated. One of the most important things to keep track of is the logins of users to your Snowflake account. It's important because if accounts are accessed by unauthorized people, it may have severe consequences, such as data leaks. In many cases, there are early signs of such occurrences:

- Sometimes attackers have incomplete information (such as a list of possible passwords), and thus, it's important to monitor failed login attempts.

- Sometimes new IP addresses connecting (or trying to connect) to the Snowflake account can indicate either attack attempts or careless behavior (such as employees or administrators who are setting a too liberal network policy for their comfort). It's important to monitor the IP addresses accessing the data warehouse, as well as the network policies, to make sure you know of such issues.

- Sometimes users are setting a relaxed authentication method, such as canceling two-factor authentication or using user-password authentication for an application (instead of key-pair authentication). It is important to monitor how access is done, and the configuration of user access, to prevent such cases, which increase the security risk on your Snowflake account.

In addition to all of that, having a control in place to audit all logins to the system is important in terms of compliance. With regard to that, you should probably consult with your organization's compliance officer or team, to understand the specific requirements, which are sometimes covered "out of the box" (by having the account usage login_history view which holds all failed and successful logins for the last year), but sometimes requires additional preparation from your end.

Examples

The following query checks for failed logins in the last ten minutes, for close monitoring:

```
SELECT event_timestamp, user_name, client_ip, reported_client_type, first_
authentication_factor, second_authentication_factor, error_code, error_
message
FROM TABLE(information_schema.login_history(
    result_limit => 10000,
  time_range_start => TIMEADD("minute", -10, CURRENT_TIMESTAMP()),
  time_range_end => CURRENT_TIMESTAMP()
))
WHERE is_success='NO';
```

The following query checks for users with the most failed logins in the last week:

```
SELECT user_name, COUNT(1) AS failed_logins
FROM snowflake.account_usage.login_history
WHERE is_success = 'NO'
AND event_timestamp >= TIMEADD("day", -7, CURRENT_TIMESTAMP())
GROUP BY 1
ORDER BY 2 DESC;
```

The following query shows the users logging in from the most IP addresses in the last week:

```
SELECT user_name, COUNT(DISTINCT client_ip) AS ips_used
FROM snowflake.account_usage.login_history
WHERE event_timestamp >= TIMEADD("day", -7, CURRENT_TIMESTAMP())
GROUP BY 1
ORDER BY 2 DESC;
```

The following query shows all IP addresses used for successful logins in the last week and not used before (depending on your Snowflake usage, this can be important on its own or may need to be filtered for specific users):

```
WITH ips_prior_usage AS (
  SELECT DISTINCT client_ip FROM snowflake.account_usage.login_history
  WHERE event_timestamp < TIMEADD("day", -7, CURRENT_TIMESTAMP())
)
SELECT DISTINCT client_ip FROM snowflake.account_usage.login_history
WHERE event_timestamp >= TIMEADD("day", -7, CURRENT_TIMESTAMP())
AND client_ip NOT IN (SELECT client_ip FROM ips_prior_usage);
```

Finding Admin Role Abuses

Another use case of monitoring your Snowflake account is to find abuse of admin roles. In many cases, the reasons for these are not maliciousness, but carelessness. It's not that an administrator doesn't care about the security of the Snowflake account, it's often simply lack of consciousness about security or careless behavior due to laziness or lack of time. This means you'd like to monitor cases such as

- Admin roles that are granted too broadly (which increases the risks based on account compromise or other careless administrative behaviors).

- Admin roles used for data queries. Often it's the case that admin roles are used as a "god mode" to be able to access anything and handle any problem, which is also increasing the risk of sensitive data being exposed to the wrong hands and is often also against compliance requirements. Admin roles should not be used for accessing data.

- Admin roles used with weak authentication or lack of network policies.

- Admin roles that are being used in scripts, especially using username and password, which increase the risk of exposure to their credentials. Note that, unfortunately, as you've seen throughout this chapter, in several cases, you will actually need to defy this when monitoring data that requires an admin role (even ACCOUNTADMIN). You need to make sure that these cases are well compensated by other means like stronger authentication, network policies, etc.

Examples

The following query returns a list of users with admin roles and their admin roles:

```
SELECT grantee_name AS user, ARRAY_AGG(role) AS roles FROM snowflake.
account_usage.grants_to_users
WHERE ROLE LIKE '%ADMIN'
AND deleted_on IS NULL
GROUP BY user;
```

The following query retrieves the SELECT queries performed by admin roles in the last week:

```
SELECT user_name, role_name, query_id, query_text, database_name, schema_name
FROM snowflake.account_usage.query_history
WHERE role_name LIKE '%ADMIN'
AND query_type = 'SELECT';
```

The following query checks for users with admin roles who has a local password configured:

```
WITH users_with_admin_roles AS (
SELECT grantee_name AS user FROM snowflake.account_usage.grants_to_users
WHERE ROLE LIKE '%ADMIN'
AND deleted_on IS NULL)
SELECT name FROM snowflake.account_usage.users
WHERE deleted_on IS NULL
AND has_password = 'TRUE'
AND name IN (SELECT user FROM users_with_admin_roles);
```

The following query finds admin roles used in sessions where the client is not the web UI (this may need to be adjusted per your specific requirements, but using an admin role from a script should **really** be controlled):

```
SELECT sessions.session_id, sessions.created_on, sessions.user_name, query_
history.role_name, sessions.client_application_id,
        login_history.client_ip FROM snowflake.account_usage.sessions
```

```
LEFT JOIN snowflake.account_usage.query_history ON (sessions.session_id =
query_history.session_id)
LEFT JOIN snowflake.account_usage.login_history ON (sessions.login_event_id
= login_history.event_id)
WHERE query_history.role_name LIKE '%ADMIN'
AND client_application_id NOT LIKE 'Snowflake UI%'
ORDER BY created_on DESC
LIMIT 100;
```

Finding admin users who are not using network policies or those that are using the ones you don't want to use is, unfortunately, not an easy task, as network policies can only be pulled by a SHOW command (not a SELECT), which can't be joined or used within a CTE (a WITH statement).

The following workaround (courtesy of Snowflake's support!) is creating a stored procedure that holds this data:

```
CREATE OR REPLACE PROCEDURE myuserlist()
  RETURNS VARCHAR NOT NULL
  LANGUAGE JAVASCRIPT
  EXECUTE AS CALLER
  AS
  $$
  var return_value = "";
  try {
     // table to store user and network policy
     command = "create or replace temporary table USER_LEVELS (username
     varchar(100),value VARCHAR(100), level VARCHAR(100));";
     snowflake.createStatement( {sqlText: command}  ).execute();
     // run command for listing users,  use the like statement to narrow
        the list if required
     var stmt = snowflake.createStatement( {sqlText: "SHOW USERS;"}  );
     stmt.execute();
     // use the previous query ID to get the list of users and put into
        user_list table
     var queryid = stmt.getQueryId();
     stmt = snowflake.createStatement(
```

```
  {sqlText: "create or replace temporary table user_list as select $1
  from table(result_scan('"+queryid+"'));"}
 );
stmt.execute();
// Now go through the user_list table and call show parameters for
   each user and put the result in USER_LEVELS table
 var command = "SELECT * FROM user_list;";
 var stmt = snowflake.createStatement( {sqlText: command } );
 var rs = stmt.execute();
 //First record
 if (rs.next())  {
     name = rs.getColumnValue(1);
     cmd = "show parameters like 'NETWORK_POLICY' for user " + name
     var stmtx = snowflake.createStatement( {sqlText: cmd}  );
     stmtx.execute();
     var queryid = stmtx.getQueryId();
     stmty = snowflake.createStatement(
        {sqlText: "insert into  USER_LEVELS select '" + name +
        "',$2,$4 from table(result_scan('"+queryid+"'));"}
        );
     stmty.execute();
 }
 // Remain records
 while (rs.next())  {
     name = rs.getColumnValue(1);
     cmd = "show parameters like 'NETWORK_POLICY' for user \"" +
     name + "\""
     var stmtx = snowflake.createStatement( {sqlText: cmd}  );
     stmtx.execute();
     var queryid = stmtx.getQueryId();
     stmty = snowflake.createStatement(
        {sqlText: "insert into  USER_LEVELS select '" + name +
        "',$2,$4 from table(result_scan('"+queryid+"'));"}
        );
```

```
        stmty.execute();
    }
}
catch (err)  {
    result =  "Failed: Code: " + err.code + "\n  State: " + err.state;
    result += "\n  Message: " + err.message;
    result += "\nStack Trace:\n" + err.stackTraceTxt;
}
return return_value;
$$
;
```

You can then use the stored procedure, as follows:

```
CALL myuserlist();
SELECT * FROM USER_LIST ORDER BY 1;
SELECT * FROM USER_LEVELS ORDER BY 1 ;
```

For retrieving a list of all network policies (as a JSON), you can use the following undocumented query:

```
SELECT ENTITY_DETAIL('NETWORK_POLICY', '', '') AS NETWORK_POLICY_DETAIL;
```

Monitoring Administrative Operations and Configuration Changes

It is important to track specific administrative operations, as these operations may indicate behavior that can increase security risks (e.g., canceling network policies). It is important mainly because in many cases, it is exactly these situations, such as a configuration change done "temporarily," that lower the level of security for the protected resources. It starts with someone with benign intentions changing something and ends in a data breach.

Some of the operations also need to be tracked as part of compliance requirements (e.g., sometimes changes in access to sensitive data needs to be tracked). This can be a requirement for an audit log for administrative operations, but can also be more specific, depending on the specific requirements of your organization.

When it comes to having an audit log of administrative operations, you can extract that as a subset of the QUERY_HISTORY, which is in the account usage schema. You can either filter this view by admin roles, by the users known to have admin roles, and by specific operations which can either be found by filtering the query_text column or in some cases by the query_type column.

In addition to parsing the query log, you can also make periodic queries on specific configuration you want to monitor, to make sure all changes are accounted for. For example, you can monitor the users table according to your security policies (e.g., make sure there are no users with weak authentication), monitor network policies for changes, dynamic masking, and so on.

Examples

The following query looks for the last 100 queries that are using a system variable:

```
SELECT query_id, user_name, start_time, query_text
FROM snowflake.account_usage.query_history
WHERE query_text ILIKE '%SYSTEM$%'
ORDER BY start_time DESC
LIMIT 100;
```

The following query looks for the last 100 queries done with the ACCOUNTADMIN role:

```
SELECT query_id, user_name, start_time, query_text
FROM snowflake.account_usage.query_history
WHERE role_name = 'ACCOUNTADMIN'
ORDER BY start_time DESC
LIMIT 100;
```

The following query looks for the last 100 queries that made changes to network policies:

```
SELECT query_id, user_name, start_time, query_text
FROM snowflake.account_usage.query_history
WHERE query_type LIKE '%NETWORK_POLICY'
ORDER BY start_time DESC
LIMIT 100;
```

The following query checks for all users created not by the USERADMIN role in the last month (which should handle user creations):

```
SELECT start_time, query_text, user_name, role_name FROM snowflake.account_
usage.query_history
WHERE query_type = 'CREATE_USER'
AND role_name != 'USERADMIN'
AND start_time > DATEADD('month', -1, CURRENT_TIMESTAMP());
```

Note   A separate monitoring rule can monitor all user creations, without the role_name filter.

The following query monitors the latest changes to time travel configuration of objects. Time travel changes may break compliance, so it's important to monitor them.

```
SELECT start_time, query_text, user_name, role_name FROM snowflake.account_
usage.query_history
WHERE query_text ILIKE '%data_retention_time_in_days%'
AND start_time > DATEADD('month', -1, CURRENT_TIMESTAMP());
```

The following query checks for changes in account-level parameters done in the last month:

```
SELECT start_time, query_text, user_name, role_name FROM snowflake.account_
usage.query_history
WHERE query_type = 'ALTER_ACCOUNT'
AND start_time > DATEADD('month', -1, CURRENT_TIMESTAMP());
```

Managing Overprivileged Users

As discussed in Chapter 6, "Authorization: Data Access Control," one of the challenges when managing privileges in Snowflake (and in general) is overprivileges. Over time, users accumulate access to data they don't need anymore (i.e., if they even needed it in the first place), which means that you're getting all the risk of data exposure, minus the value which balances this trade-off. We went through this in length, suggesting options like different role management strategies and self-service access provisioning.

However, either before or after you're implementing processes to lower the amount of overprivileged users, you should try to find out where you're standing and monitor the situation. This means that you'd like to know answers to questions such as

- Which roles are not used by any user and can be dropped?

- Which roles are not used by specific users and can be revoked?

- Which tables are not being accessed by users, despite having access to them?

It is not always straightforward to find the answers to these questions. Sometimes the role hierarchy makes it difficult to find the answers to some of these questions, which requires recursively checking privileges for a user to know the answers to such questions. In other cases, there are access control policies "hidden" within views to create row- or column-based access control policies. The point here is not to despair you, our dear reader! It is simply to reiterate that some things can be a bit more complicated to solve and that you need to take into account the architecture of your Snowflake account.

Another challenge is knowing which tables were used in each query, so that you can know whether or not they've been used by a certain user or using a certain role. Currently, this requires parsing the query itself, to extract the tables (which is not a simple task). Snowflake is also working on a more granular logging which will include this information.

Examples

The following query checks for unused roles in the last six months. Note that it's ignoring role hierarchy, which may need to be taken into account, depending on your role architecture. If so, you will need to expand on this.

```
WITH used_roles AS (
  SELECT DISTINCT role_name FROM snowflake.account_usage.query_history
  WHERE start_time > DATEADD("month", -6, CURRENT_TIMESTAMP())
)
SELECT name FROM snowflake.account_usage.roles
WHERE deleted_on IS NULL
AND name NOT IN (SELECT role_name FROM used_roles);
```

The following query checks which roles are privileged to a user, but unused in the last six months by the user (note that if you're using this at scale, it may be very slow due to query_history being a huge table; you may want to copy it to a different table, or create a slimmer summary of it instead):

```
WITH all_grants AS (
  SELECT created_on, role AS role_name, grantee_name AS user_name
  FROM snowflake.account_usage.grants_to_users
  WHERE deleted_on IS NULL
),
last_used_roles AS (
  SELECT role_name, user_name, MAX(start_time) AS last_query_time
  FROM snowflake.account_usage.query_history
  WHERE start_time > DATEADD("month", -6, CURRENT_TIMESTAMP())
  GROUP BY 1, 2
)
SELECT all_grants.user_name, all_grants.role_name FROM
    all_grants LEFT JOIN last_used_roles ON
    (all_grants.role_name = last_used_roles.role_name
    AND all_grants.user_name = last_used_roles.user_name)
    WHERE last_used_roles.last_query_time IS NULL;
```

Monitoring Usage of Vulnerable Drivers

Another use case for monitoring can be to monitor access to the system, which is done from vulnerable driver versions. From time to time, security vulnerabilities are found in software, and monitoring access done by vulnerable drivers can help you to easily pinpoint the users who are using the outdated drivers and ask them nicely to update their drivers.

For up-to-date information, you can look in the release notes of the drivers or attempt to make sure users are using the latest versions.

The following query gets the users with the driver versions they were using in the last week:

```
SELECT user_name, reported_client_type || ' ' || reported_client_version AS
driver, COUNT(1) AS logins FROM snowflake.account_usage.login_history
WHERE event_timestamp > DATEADD('week', -1, CURRENT_TIMESTAMP())
```

```
AND driver NOT LIKE 'SNOWFLAKE_UI%'
GROUP BY 1, 2
ORDER BY 1;
```

This can be augmented by joining with grants_to_users, to prioritize users with administrative roles, or be limited to a specific set of versions.

7.3. Object Tagging

The topic of object tagging (which, at the time of writing, is still in preview) can be used for several things, but we thought it would be interesting to mention it as it can be very useful for monitoring, as well as for other uses like applying smarter data access control.

Object tags are key-value pairs, which can be applied to securable objects like databases, schemas, and virtual data warehouses, but even to specific columns. That way you can add a lot of metadata context to your Snowflake objects, and either use that in policies or in reports and monitoring.

A good example is using object tagging to tag specific columns based on the type of data they have. For example, you may tag columns by types of PII that they hold. Then you can apply reporting which can increase your security and governance, such as looking at tables with PII that have public access or many other use cases.

To create new tags, you use the CREATE TAG command, as follows:

```
CREATE TAG PII_TYPE;
```

You can then apply the tag using the following command:

```
ALTER TABLE promotions.candyclub.users
MODIFY COLUMN user_email
SET TAG pii_type='email';
```

You can then use the new tag_references account usage view for monitoring. For example, the following query checks for columns tagged as email, without an email dynamic policy applied on them:

```
WITH column_with_tag AS
(
SELECT ref_entity_name AS table_name, ref_column_name AS column_name,
  ref_database_name AS db_name, ref_schema_name AS schema_name
```

```
FROM snowflake.account_usage.tag_references
WHERE tag_name = 'PII_TYPE'
AND column_tag_value = 'email'),
column_with_policy AS (
SELECT ref_entity_name AS table_name, ref_column_name AS column_name,
  ref_database_name AS db_name, ref_schema_name AS schema_name
FROM TABLE(information_schema.policy_references('security_policies.masking_
policies.email_mask')))
SELECT * FROM column_with_tag
EXCEPT
SELECT * FROM column_with_policy;
```

Though this feature is still in preview, we feel like there are going to be a lot of innovative ways to use it, to gain great operational and security value.

7.4. How to Monitor?

Now that we discussed the relevant information you can pull from Snowflake and some of the prominent use cases for monitoring and auditing your Snowflake account, a question that remains unanswered is how exactly to monitor this data. Obviously, if you're looking at the data in an ad hoc manner, for example, when doing an incident response, you can use Snowflake's web UI or your favorite database client or data analytics tool. However, when setting up your infrastructure for an ongoing monitoring of your Snowflake account's security, it's time to make something more stable that continuously gives you the visibility, availability, and alerting capabilities so you're always on top of your Snowflake account's security.

7.4.1. Using Tasks to Prepare Data

Sometimes you may want to use Snowflake tasks to prepare data. There are several reasons for doing that. You may want to prepare audit tables with specific data ready in them, such as a table with a log of all admin actions (which is a subset of query_history). You may want to have a table recording a snapshot of certain configurations periodically.

Another common use case is to copy large tables like query_history and login_ history from the account usage schema to a different location. This can be done so that further analysis can be done with a separate non-admin role, in case you want to save the data for longer retention periods than one year or in case you want to run analysis on the data (in account usage, it is quite sluggish).

Snowflake tasks are a very strong engine for such ongoing activities such as ETLs and maintenance, and in case you want to learn more about it, you can visit Snowflake's documentation. However, here are a couple of examples for such tasks, which you can customize to your needs.

Examples

First, let's create admin_actions and query_history tables in the acme_admin.monitoring schema:

```
CREATE DATABASE IF NOT EXISTS acme_admin;
CREATE SCHEMA IF NOT EXISTS acme_admin.monitoring;
CREATE TABLE acme_admin.monitoring.admin_actions
LIKE snowflake.account_usage.query_history;
CREATE TABLE acme_admin.monitoring.query_history
LIKE snowflake.account_usage.query_history;
```

The following query sets a task that copies the entire query_history table from the previous day to the acme_admin.monitoring.query_history table, every day at 04:00am UTC:

```
CREATE TASK queries_duplication
  WAREHOUSE = compute_wh
  SCHEDULE = 'USING CRON 0 4 * * * UTC'
  TIMESTAMP_INPUT_FORMAT = 'YYYY-MM-DD HH24'
AS
INSERT INTO acme_admin.monitoring.query_history
SELECT * FROM snowflake.account_usage.query_history
WHERE start_time > DATEADD("day", -1, CURRENT_DATE());

ALTER TASK queries_duplication RESUME;
```

The following query sets a task that copies only admin actions (actions performed by admin roles, though your requirements may be different, such as to filter by query_type) from the previous day to the acme_admin.monitoring.admin_actions table, every day at 05:00am UTC:

```
CREATE TASK admin_actions_duplication
  WAREHOUSE = compute_wh
  SCHEDULE = 'USING CRON 0 5 * * * UTC'
  TIMESTAMP_INPUT_FORMAT = 'YYYY-MM-DD HH24'
AS
INSERT INTO acme_admin.monitoring.admin_actions_duplication
SELECT * FROM snowflake.account_usage.query_history
WHERE start_time > DATEADD("day", -1, CURRENT_DATE())
AND role_name LIKE '%ADMIN';

ALTER TASK admin_actions_duplication RESUME;
```

7.4.2. Building a Snowsight Security Dashboard

There are many different ways in which you can consume Snowflake data as part of data analytics, and we all have our favorite tools, whether it's exporting the data to a Splunk or ELK, or integrating with a SIEM (Security Information and Events Management). One might argue that instead of pulling the data from Snowflake, you should actually push the logs from other security controls to your Snowflake (for more information, read Chapter 9, "Snowflake for Security").

If you choose to pull the data and display it in another dashboarding or analytics platform, you can feel free to do so if that works for you. However, another cool solution is to build your Snowflake security dashboard in Snowflake itself, using Snowsight. To log into your Snowsight (which is available in all Snowflake account levels), go to https:// app.snowflake.com, and continue with the OAuth login.

Once inside Snowsight, go to the Dashboards menu item, and add a new dashboard, using the + **Dashboard** button. Let's call this new dashboard "Security Dashboard," and click **Create Dashboard**.

Once we're inside the new dashboard, we can add tiles to the dashboard with different visualizations we'd like to see in our security dashboard. Of course, you can customize the dashboard based on the data we've seen in this chapter, per your liking and needs, but let's get started with a few tiles.

Failed Logins Tile

In the first tile, we will set a tile to display the top login failures, grouped by usernames and failure reasons. To do that, put the following query in the tile's query box:

```
SELECT CONCAT(user_name, ' (', error_message, ')') AS User, COUNT(*) AS
failures FROM snowflake.account_usage.login_history WHERE event_timestamp =
:daterange
AND is_success = 'NO'
GROUP BY user_name, error_message
ORDER BY failures DESC
LIMIT 10
```

As you can see, the query contains the filter event_timestamp = :daterange, which is a placeholder that changes to a time range filter, according to the date range selection in the dashboard; for example, it may change to

```
(event_timestamp >= ('2022-01-01 13:31:27')::timestamp
AND event_timestamp < ('2022-01-14 13:31:27')::timestamp)
```

In the tile editor, choose Chart. At the time of writing, sadly, Snowsight has no pie chart or donut pie chart, so we will resort to displaying the results as a bar chart. Choose the bar chart from the Chart Type drop-down menu. In the x-axis, choose User to display the correct labels and the horizontal bars orientation. Finally, change the tile's title to "Top Login Failures," and return to the security dashboard, to add the next tile.

Users Connecting from the Most IPs Tile

Now let's either duplicate and edit the chart, or create a new one and customize it in the same way, to create another title, displaying the users who are connected from the most IP addresses:

```
SELECT user_name AS User, COUNT(DISTINCT client_ip) AS IPs FROM snowflake.
account_usage.login_history WHERE event_timestamp = :daterange
GROUP BY user_name, error_message
ORDER BY IPs DESC
LIMIT 10
```

Users with Admin Roles Tile

Let's add another tile, this time displaying a list of all users with an admin role enabled, and this time, set this tile as a grid, not a chart:

```
SELECT grantee_name AS user
FROM snowflake.account_usage.grants_to_users
WHERE deleted_on IS NULL
AND role LIKE '%ADMIN%';
```

As you can see, these are examples, and you can add more tiles with information that will be helping you monitor the security of your Snowflake account, either from the examples throughout this chapter or from your own customizations. And if you think of some additional ones with great value, we'd love to hear. Also, if you're looking for more information about how to work with Snowsight, you can go to Snowflake's documentation.

7.5. Alerting

Last but not least, having tables with data and a dashboard to display them is sweet, but sometimes you want to know when something happens that requires your attention. In those cases, you'd like to send out alerts to those responsible for the security of your Snowflake security, whether that's you or others. You can start at some level of notification (even, yikes, an email) and continue from there as you mature this project to using APIs to send alerts via Slack, open tickets on Jira, or interface with other services like ServiceNow.

Examples to such alerts can be found throughout this chapter, but some examples are notifications when

- There's a new admin role grant.

- There's a change in network policies, or in their assignment to the account or to specific users.

- There's an admin role usage for selecting data (be careful not to flood yourself with this one).

- There are changes in column security definitions.

- There are changes in SCIM configuration or generation of tokens.

- There is a repeating login failure for a user.

You can find more examples throughout this chapter, or you can create your own relevant ones.

Here are some ways in which you can implement these notifications.

7.5.1. Using Custom Scripting

One way to do so is to write an application that periodically queries Snowflake and, depending on the results, triggers the workflow you'd like to trigger (such as send an API call to an application that will send out a notification or open a ticket). This is a pretty straightforward way, and you'd run it in the same way you're running other similar applications, using any scripting language, with its Snowflake connector. Of course, when you're connecting and performing these checks, make sure you're doing in a secure way (as per Chapter 4, "Authentication: Keeping Strangers Out"), by using a key-pair authentication.

7.5.2. Using Tasks and External Functions

Another way to send out the notifications is to set up tasks that utilize external functions. In the external functions, you implement the logic that triggers the workflow according to the values sent by the queries. To do that, use the CREATE TASK for creating the repeating task and CREATE EXTERNAL FUNCTION. However, keep in mind that though this seems to be a quick, almost self-contained process, it requires creating an API integration (which is currently supported in AWS, Azure, and GCP where the last is still in preview at the time of writing) and splitting the logic between the tasks and the code to verify the results. That is why this is less recommended.

7.5.3. Using SnowAlert

The third way is by using SnowAlert, an open source project by Snowflake, which enables sending alerts over Snowflake query results, as well as over data ingested into Snowflake from other systems. You can learn more about SnowAlert in Chapter 9, "Snowflake for Security."

7.6. Using Third-Party Vendors for Monitoring, Auditing, and Alerting

As you can see, Snowflake provides quite an extensive platform for getting valuable data that helps you to audit your activity, monitor your account's security, and alert you whenever you want to get notifications. However, there are several third-party solutions that can help with that, either by building on top of what Snowflake has, by orchestrating the abilities, or by controlling the data access and enriching it with additional context from other controls like your IdP or other systems.

Using third-party vendors may be saving you a lot of resources, to free you up for doing other things, and analyzing the advantages and disadvantages of each solution is beyond the scope of this book.

7.7. Summary

In this chapter, we went through a lot of metadata which can be extracted from Snowflake and how you can leverage this data to meet compliance requirements and make sure your security risk is monitored and under control. We realize that this is a lot of information to process, which can be translated into great visibility and additional security for you and your users. We also realize that you're a busy person and that you have a lot to do.

That is why, our recommendation is to prioritize and start with basic monitoring capabilities and continue to mature from there onward.

CHAPTER 8

Secure Data Sharing with Snowflake

An important part of a modern data ecosystem in many cases is the ability to share data between different teams and with others within or outside of your organization. The latter is especially interesting, as almost all companies are now sharing data with other companies (suppliers, customers, partners, service providers, government agencies, and more), and data sharing is often done in a suboptimal way from both an operational and a security perspective.

Let's discuss the different methods of data sharing in Snowflake and the security guidelines for each one.

8.1. Direct Share

The basic way to share data with other Snowflake accounts is to use direct share or secure data sharing. When you want to share objects with other accounts, you need to create a ***share*** object, which you can think of as a specific type of role, to which you can grant privileges. Similar to roles, if you want to give the share access to tables, views, and other objects within a schema, you must provide it with a usage grant on the database and schema.

The following query will create a share for ACME Candies' ingredients buying predictions with ACME candy ingredients, a supplier of ACME Candies:

```
CREATE SHARE ingredient_predictions;

GRANT USAGE ON DATABASE manufacturing TO SHARE ingredient_predictions;
GRANT USAGE ON SCHEMA manufacturing.goods TO SHARE ingredient_predictions;
GRANT SELECT ON TABLE manufacturing.goods.buying_predictions TO SHARE
ingredient_predictions;

ALTER SHARE ingredient_predictions ADD accounts=acme_ingredients;
```

© Ben Herzberg, Yoav Cohen 2022
B. Herzberg and Y. Cohen, *Snowflake Security*, https://doi.org/10.1007/978-1-4842-7389-0_8

Some notes about secure data sharing:

1. Since a share can only share tables and secure views from a single database, if you want to share objects from different databases using one share, you will need to add corresponding views in a single database.

2. Shares must be in the same region. If you want to share data to a different region, you need to first replicate the database to another account you control in the region of the data-consuming account.

3. Sharing data with other accounts may impact your compliance. For example, if you are HIPAA compliant, you need to sign a BAA (business associate agreement) with the data consumer (or data provider, if you are the data consumer).

4. As the data provider, you will not get any logging of the queries running against the shared data. This may be a security concern.

5. Data sharing works even if you have tri-secret configured on your account. If you have tri-secret and revoke your key, this will of course prevent using the shared data from that point forward.

8.1.1. Consuming Shared Data

When you are consuming data, whether it's a shared table or other shared objects, as we will see in the following. When a share is shared with you, you can either create a database for it from the UI (under Shares ➤ Inbound) or run the following SQL query; in this case it's ACME Candies accepting campaigns data from their partners, ACME Savories:

```
CREATE DATABASE "CAMPAIGNS_FROM_SAVORIES"
FROM SHARE ACMESAVORIES."CAMPAIGNS_SHARED_WITH_CANDIES" COMMENT='Shared
campaigns data from ACME savories';
GRANT IMPORTED PRIVILEGES ON DATABASE "CAMPAIGNS_FROM_SAVORIES" TO ROLE
"ANALYST_DIRECTOR";
```

A couple of security guidelines when consuming data from your partners:

1. Consider this data as data you don't control, for example, when making use of it in internal systems, make sure you treat input as unsanitized. As an example, don't assume that data imported is filtered against XSS (cross-site scripting) payloads, so if you display the data in internal systems, make sure you properly escape it (as you should with other data, of course).

2. If this data contains sensitive information, such as PII, make sure you are aware of it and are mapping access to the sensitive data, as you would with regular sensitive data.

8.1.2. Sharing Partial Data Using Secure Objects

In many cases, you want to share partial data with the data consumer. For example, ACME Candies may want to share a table with employees' data with a company handling payrolls, but not share all the data about those employees, just the relevant columns.

In another case, ACME Candies may want to share purchase orders with its suppliers. The purchase orders are in one table, but ACME wants each supplier to only get the purchasing orders belonging to them.

Let's discuss the different ways to share this data in a secure way.

Using Secure Views

Let's discuss the first case, of sharing only partial data from the employees' table. We will use a secure view to share only specific columns from the table. A secure view is a view where even users with select access to the object can't view its logic, and it also eliminates some of the optimizations, to prevent getting answers about data you shouldn't be able to access by means like timing queries.

When you grant access to a view, you don't need to grant select access to the underlying asset as well, meaning that if you share the secure view, the data-consuming account will not be able to see the data you don't want to share. Assuming we already have a share called share_salaries, let's set this up:

```
CREATE SECURE VIEW v_payrolls AS
SELECT first_name, last_name, bank_account, current_salary
FROM employees;

GRANT SELECT ON v_payrolls TO SHARE share_salaries;
```

Note that in the same way in which you create a secure view, you can create a secure materialized view. Materialized views are pre-computed views, and more information about them can be found in Snowflake documentation.

Using Dynamic Secure Views

Let's consider the second case, where we want to apply row-level security and share each supplier with the purchase orders belonging to them. In this case, we can set up a separate secure view for each supplier, which is going to be redundant and ugly. Instead, we can use the supplier account as a contextual parameter, which we can filter the results by.

Suppose we don't want to pollute the purchase_orders table with the Snowflake account IDs of our suppliers, we can create a mapping table containing the mapping between account IDs and supplier IDs (or supplier names). Based on this, we can make a dynamic view to pull data based on the account ID and only for pending orders.

Let's first create some mock data. Here are the mock tables and data, in case you want to try this out:

```
CREATE TABLE map_suppliers (supplier_id integer, account_id text);
INSERT INTO map_suppliers VALUES (1, CURRENT_ACCOUNT());
CREATE TABLE purchase_orders (product_id integer, product_name text,
quantity integer, order_status integer, supplier_id integer);
INSERT INTO purchase_orders VALUES (1, 'test', 5, 2, 1);
```

And now let's create the secure view, using the entitlement mapping to provide dynamically filtered content:

```
CREATE SECURE VIEW v_purchase_orders AS
SELECT product_id, product_name, quantity
FROM purchase_orders
JOIN map_suppliers ON (purchase_orders.supplier_id = map_suppliers.
supplier_id)
WHERE order_status = 2 -- pending
AND map_suppliers.account_id = CURRENT_ACCOUNT();
```

Using Secure UDFs

Suppose you want to be even more restrictive than giving a filtered secure view. This may be due to the need to share data, but to restrict wide-scale access (such as the data consumer pulling the entire dataset). It may also be when you want to provide the data but now allow the data consumers to apply aggregations on the entire data set.

In this case, your next option is to use secure UDFs (user-defined functions). When dealing with secure functions, as with secure views, the consumer does not require access to the underlying data, and even further than that, you can limit them to pull data based on certain dimensions, which will limit their ability to access your data. For example, you may implement a function that returns data that is only relevant for a specific time, specific product, etc.

Let's say, for example, that ACME Candies wants to expose a function to their retail partners, which will return a list of the upcoming allowed discounts on their candies. As they don't want a rogue retailer running a "SELECT *" query on the exposed data and having access to all the discounts they provide on all product lines, they may implement it as the get_discounts_for_product function, which accepts a product ID as a parameter.

To do that, let's first add the mock future discounts table:

```
CREATE DATABASE sales;
CREATE SCHEMA sales.retail;
CREATE TABLE sales.retail.future_discounts
(product_id integer, from_date timestamp, to_date timestamp, discount_
amount integer);
```

```
INSERT INTO  sales.retail.future_discounts VALUES
(1, CURRENT_TIMESTAMP(), DATEADD('day', 7, CURRENT_TIMESTAMP()), 25);

USE sales.retail;
```

Now, let's add the shared UDF:

```
CREATE SECURE FUNCTION
get_future_discounts_for_product(input_product_id integer)
RETURNS TABLE (from_date timestamp, to_date timestamp, discount_amount
integer)
AS
'SELECT from_date, to_date, discount_amount
FROM sales.retail.future_discounts
WHERE product_id = input_product_id';
```

Running the following query will return the discounts for product ID 1:

```
SELECT * FROM TABLE(GET_FUTURE_DISCOUNTS_FOR_PRODUCT(1));
```

And now all we need to do is to share this function with the retail partners, for their delight:

```
CREATE SHARE IF NOT EXISTS retail_partners;
GRANT USAGE ON DATABASE sales TO SHARE retail_partners;
GRANT USAGE ON SCHEMA sales.retail TO SHARE retail_partners;
GRANT USAGE ON FUNCTION sales.retail.get_future_discounts_for_
product(integer) TO SHARE retail_partners;
ALTER SHARE retail_partners ADD ACCOUNTS = retailer1, retailer2;
```

Note that while this method gives you more control over what you share and under what dimensions you're providing the data, it is not bulletproof in its current form. The retailers in this sample can still write a script that retrieves all products from 1 to n (also known as scraping the data). Since usage of shared UDFs is logged in the consumers' account, not in the provider account, you will not know it.

Given that, this will both require them to do some work explicitly to break your sharing terms and add expenses on their end (e.g., instead of running one query of SELECT ... INTO, they will need to run millions of queries). In other words, it's all a matter of risk and may suffice in many cases. After all, you *do* want to share this data, so it's not business secrets, but you're making it significantly harder to abuse your kind will. However, unlike exposing an API for the same usage, sharing a UDF is much easier to set up, and no external components are needed.

Using Secure Joins

Another form of secure sharing is secure joins. Unlike secure views and secure UDFs, this is not a SQL extension (SELECT * FROM tbl1 SECURE JOIN tbl2); rather it's a combination of secure functions used to securely join shared data, limiting the exposure of the data shared.

Secure joins are useful in situations where you want to get an understanding of joined items between a data provider and a data consumer, without exposing the group of items themselves. As an example, it may be when you want to check what common customers two companies have, without one of the companies exposing their customer base to the other companies. As you can see, this is a concept or an implementation of secure UDFs, and expanding on this concept can solve tough data sharing problems. The idea of secure joins is to create a joined key for the private items, and this key is a combination of hashed values that prevents de-anonymization of the shared data.

As an example, let's say that ACME Candies wants to run a Valentine's campaign with one of its partners, ACME Savories. To better understand the effect of this collaboration, ACME Candies wants to better understand the overlapping users between the companies, as represented (for the purposes of this example) by a list of email addresses.

For simplicity, we will run this demo under one account, but the only difference is that you also need to create a share, which grants access to the secure functions, as per the last section. So let's start with creating two tables, with examples of emails for the two companies:

```
CREATE TABLE acme_candies (email string);
CREATE TABLE acme_savories (email string);

INSERT INTO acme_candies VALUES ('a@a.com'), ('b@b.com'), ('c@c.com'),
('d@d.com'), ('e@e.com');
INSERT INTO acme_savories VALUES ('c@c.com'), ('d@d.com'), ('e@e.com'),
('f@f.com'), ('g@g.com');
```

Next, let's create a function that generates the hashed join key:

```
CREATE SECURE FUNCTION get_join_key(email string)
RETURNS string AS
'
SHA2(email || SHA2(CURRENT_ACCOUNT() || \'<some salt>\'))
';
```

As you can see, we concatenate (using the || operator) the email which was the input, along with the hash of the account running the function, and a salt we (as the data provider) add, and then we hash (using SHA256, but of course any hashing algorithm can work here) and return the results. This means that the key is different for each data item (email), but also is different for each account, and with the added salt (known only to the provider, ACME Candies), making it uniquely created only by the provider.

The second function we (ACME Candies) create is the following:

```
CREATE SECURE FUNCTION secure_lookup(join_key string, consumer_salt string)
RETURNS numeric(10)
AS
'
SELECT COUNT(*)
FROM acme_candies
WHERE join_key = SHA2(IFNULL(email, to_char(random())) || consumer_salt ||
SHA2(CURRENT_ACCOUNT() || \'<some salt>\'))
';
```

What we've done here is to perform a count which looks up a join key (which we will generate from the get_join_key function) and match it with results from our ACME Candies' users. We're creating the concatenation here as well with the same algorithm as in get_join_key, and of course, we can't pre-compute this, as the results are dynamically created per account (due to the CURRENT_ACCOUNT() added to the hash). This means that if you're customizing the hash generation in get_join_key, you need to customize the condition in secure_lookup as well.

Now, in ACME Savories, we're adding the following function and a temporary table with the overlapping data:

```
CREATE FUNCTION get_customer_key (email string, consumer_salt string)
RETURNS STRING AS
'
IFNULL(email, to_char(random())) || consumer_salt
';

CREATE OR REPLACE TEMPORARY TABLE joinkeys AS
SELECT
get_join_key(get_customer_key(email, '<some consumer salt>')) AS join_key
FROM acme_savories;
```

The temporary table now holds hashed customer identifiers from ACME Savories' side (the consumer side), and now we're finally able to run the following query in the consumer side, which can find the amount of overlapping consumers without being exposed to the other company's data:

```
SELECT SUM(secure_lookup(join_key, '<some consumer salt>')) AS overlapping_
customers,
COUNT(*) AS total_customers, ((overlapping_customers / total_customers) *
100) AS overlap_percent
FROM joinkeys;
```

The preceding query should return an overlap of three customers and 60% overlap.

The concept of secure joins is pretty cool and can also change, according to the specific use case you're trying to solve. It also is a bit advanced, and we recommend trying the logic first on a single account, before sharing, so that it would be easier to first get to a working algorithm, before ironing out the administrative side of sharing the functions. If you want to learn more about secure joins, as well as see additional use cases, we recommend this blogpost on Snowflake's website.

8.2. Data Exchange and the Snowflake Data Marketplace

Snowflake's data exchange builds on top of the data sharing we've discussed so far in this chapter and leverages these capabilities to expose datasets that you want to share, either within or outside of your organization. It enables you to set up listings of datasets that you would like to share and manage it as a data catalog or data mart, where other accounts can get this shared data. The Snowflake data marketplace is a public listing, based on the data exchange, that enables you to publicly offer such data listings, either for free or for a price.

Having a data exchange can help you simplify data sharing of your Snowflake data, and by doing that, you can enjoy the following benefits:

1. You can have an internal "data mart," which can simplify authorization of data between your organization's groups (e.g., ACME operations can push data about the upcoming shipments around the world, and ACME marketing can consume that information and act upon). As we've seen in Chapter 6, "Authorization: Data Access Control," one of the most important things about a secure authorization of data is to have a clear policy about who can access what, and this can simplify that.

2. You can have an ecosystem with your partners (suppliers, customers, and others) and remove risks of ad hoc projects by clearly defining datasets that you feel comfortable providing to them, with a clear process of how to get that.

3. In case you have data that you're comfortable sharing publicly, you can even share it publicly using the data marketplace.

8.2.1. Managing Data Exchange

Currently, setting up data exchange for your accounts is a manual process (you open it by opening a support ticket requesting to do so), and managing listings and accepting shares are supported only by using Snowflake's new web UI (`https://app.snowflake.com`). At the time of writing, data exchange is still a preview feature, so expect more details about how to operate this and about guidelines on operation in a secure way to update over time, when this feature becomes publicly available.

A couple of security guidelines when using data exchange:

1. Once shared, you will not know the queries running on your data. That means that in your listings, you should follow the secure objects usage from earlier in this chapter. For example, prefer sharing using a secure view over sharing directly an object to be able to control what exact data you want to share, apply dynamic

filtering if needed, and use secure functions when you want to limit data retrieval even more.

2. Even if you've limited usage and dimensions over data using functions (as per the secure functions section), keep in mind that given the right incentive, the data can probably get scraped (depending on the other side's willingness to go that way and spend those resources and depending on the exact implementation). That does not mean that this is bad, it just means that you should be aware of this in the risk assessment of such a project.

3. If your compliance requirements are such that you must have logs of access to the shared data, this is not included in the data sharing (as data shared is logged in the data consumer end, not in the data provider end). A "workaround" here may be if the data consumer enables a secure view of filtered data from their query_history account usage view (see Chapter 7, "Auditing and Monitoring," for more information on that), but this depends on the use case.

4. You should, of course, be even more aware of the data sharing risks in the public Snowflake data marketplace, as instead of working with selected partners (or even teams inside an organization), you are offering the data publicly. You should make sure that what you're sharing is completely anonymized and contains no sensitive data that you don't wish to share and consider the option (mentioned in the earlier section regarding secure functions) of data scraping, before you enable public access to the data.

8.3. Reader Accounts

Up until now, we've discussed sharing of data between Snowflake accounts. But what if ACME Candies wants to share data with one of their partners who does not have a Snowflake account? Or what if ACME wants to share data while having complete visibility into all data access done on the shared data? For doing that, you will use reader accounts.

When you are creating reader accounts, instead of sharing data with an existing Snowflake account, you are creating a managed account, managed by your organization. This account, as the name suggests, can only read data, but otherwise is a fully functional account (users, roles, authentication, etc.). As a managed account, they are not signing a contract with Snowflake, and you, as the provider, are responsible for all billing. That means that it may be necessary to have some sort of a contract between the provider and the consumer, to make sure that everything is well understood.

As an example, ACME Candies would like to share some data with ACME transport, which is not a Snowflake customer. The following query creates the reader account:

```
CREATE MANAGED ACCOUNT reader_transport
ADMIN_NAME = karl_herz,
ADMIN_PASSWORD = '<hard password>',
TYPE = reader;
```

Once the account is created, you should share data with it (using the secure data sharing concepts in this chapter). Unlike normal shares, you can audit and monitor the activity of the reader accounts. The metadata is visible to you, instead of the account_usage schema, in the reader_account_usage section, which holds operational monitoring views, as well as the query_history and login_history which we discussed in Chapter 7, "Auditing and Monitoring." What this means is that, for example, if you want to monitor access to sensitive data and some of this data is in reader accounts, you will need to monitor it in the same way you're monitoring the account usage data.

The command will return the account name and login URL for the reader account, which you can share (along with the credentials) to the data consumer. They should also be responsible about their account security, in terms of making sure they apply strong authentication, data authorization if needed, etc. (you can always gift them with this book :)).

8.4. Distributed Data Clean Rooms

You can think of a distributed data clean room as a capsule that exists between two companies (or two entities within the same organization), where data processing of shared data can be done. A distributed data clean room is basically taking the secure data sharing capabilities we discussed so far, such as secure functions, secure joins, and a secure data exchange, and putting it all together.

This means that, as an example, if ACME Candies wants to have a go-to market activity with another company, where they want to work together on data of shared customers, they do so in a buffered shared environment, where the data is accessed after using secure joins, secure functions, or both, according to the type of activity the companies want to do, and where the data can then be processed by data analysts. To top it all off, of course you can add protection by using dynamic data masking and row-based policies to protect sensitive data.

This enables such organizations to privately share data, while still being compliant with data privacy and protection frameworks and regulations. The concept of data clean rooms will probably gain more features over time, for example, setting rate limiting on queries of data, and more controls.

8.5. Summary

Snowflake is built to enable secure data sharing, as it's a data platform where the metadata is centralized, making it easy to perform cross-account activities. In this chapter, we've looked into the different ways in which you can securely share data within and outside of an organization. Some of the ways to share data are answering specific use cases (such as sharing data without exposing sensitive data), and it is important to understand the concepts, so you can choose the right data sharing method with regard to the value you're trying to drive.

CHAPTER 9

Snowflake for Security

Throughout this book, we focused on operating Snowflake in a secure way. This chapter is a bit different, in which we'd like to discuss using Snowflake as a security data lake to enable better security across the enterprise. We will discuss how we got to the point that it makes sense to have a security data store (we will do this briefly, as the evolution of security controls deserves its own book) and what makes Snowflake a good choice for such purposes. We will also show a practical approach to getting started.

9.1. How We Got Here

In a typical organization, in the beginning of the century (i.e., in case you're reading this book in the 21st century), you had a handful of security controls. You probably had a firewall, an antivirus on your computers, and perhaps a bunch of other security controls. The data coming from these controls could easily be checked.

Thinking about what happened since then is dazzling – public cloud, mobile devices, IoT, big data, machine learning, AI, as well as other business and technological advancements changed the attack surface of organizations. For example, you did not need mobile device management when you had no mobile devices, and when data is relatively centralized and on a smaller scale, it is more simple to secure.

In addition, there is more of a financial incentive to attack organizations and individuals using cyber attacks (to put it simply, more money to be made). All of this brought with it a large growth in cyber attacks, as well as a growing number of security controls of different types.

A lot of these security controls are providing data about security events, but when you have dozens of such security controls in your organization, you can't have an expert dedicated to each one, and you need a consolidated way to view and react to security events.

© Ben Herzberg, Yoav Cohen 2022
B. Herzberg and Y. Cohen, *Snowflake Security*, https://doi.org/10.1007/978-1-4842-7389-0_9

9.1.1. In Comes SIEM

A SIEM (Security Information and Events Management) is a system that is used to aggregate and manage information and events from several sources, being your security controls. The idea is that events can be handled in a centralized manner, and you can create logic on top of that with correlation rules to help identify attacks across several security controls and regain control of your organization's security.

Over time, SIEM systems evolved, as part of the challenge became an alert flood, which in turn caused alert fatigue in organizations. When organizations sometimes receive 100,000s of security events each day, looking at each event individually is not feasible and does not scale, and so, there became a need to handle security events in scale, to make sure that the security events are handled, and to find indicators of more severe events that may indicate that more resources are needed to investigate or respond to a certain incident.

9.1.2. Snowflake As a Security Data Lake

So, after having this brief, fast-forward introduction to the evolution of security controls, we got to a point where we have a lot of controls in our organization, which can all give us a lot of data, but it's not easy to take this data and convert it to actual security value. This means that if you pour this data to a data platform that allows different individuals and teams to use it flexibly, you can make value of the data:

- Extracting logs and creating dashboards and reports about security events can be done within a query or a set of queries.

- Investigation into specific incidents from millions of events can also be done in a more simple way, reducing the time required to achieve results.

- Creating alerting can become very flexible, with SQL queries that can alert when certain conditions are met.

- More users can apply more data-driven approaches to solve security problems, such as detection of risky events.

- Integration with other services such as threat intelligence, either as input or as output, is easy when the data is already in a data platform.

The amount of value you can extract from consolidating your data to a data processing platform depends on the security analytics capabilities you have in your organization – security analysts and security analytics products.

9.2. Why Snowflake for a Security Data Lake

Given all of the above, it makes sense that you'd like to consolidate your security data and perform analytics on it. There are several reasons why Snowflake is a good platform to do that on. Let's discuss some of them.

9.2.1. Ease of Integration

Snowflake is easy to pour data into, either as an ad hoc import of data or setting up a continuous data pipeline. Because you have a lot of different security controls, integration times are important, and since the integration of data into Snowflake is relatively fast and simple, it reduces a lot of overhead from such a project.

9.2.2. Scalability and Features

Snowflake is easy to scale up – no additional clusters to install when you grow, no need to change your table's structures, etc. It also supports a lot of analytical and data science functions as well as can be expanded by adding functions. It connects easily to different BI tools. This is what makes Snowflake ideal for other data analytics applications as well, but it manifests itself when working on a security data platform as well.

9.2.3. Enrichments with Data Marketplace Sources

The Snowflake data marketplace allows you to quickly add data from multiple sources and add them to your queries, reporting, etc. For example, instead of building an application that adds IP addresses mapping to countries and ASNs, you can consume this data from the data marketplace and use it joined with your event data. You can add to that more data about attacking IP addresses, and you can get a better knowledge of the security events and which ones may be related or the most important to handle.

As Snowflake is making a lot of effort into adding additional data sources to the data marketplace, it looks like in the future we will have more security data to choose from in the marketplace. Think, for example, of how it may simplify file analysis if you have different information about their hashed values and more information about domains and other IoCs (indicators of compromise).

Another example, from our personal experience, is how Satori's customers can consume data from our data marketplace listing, to create self-service dashboards on security and operational issues, such as which individuals are accessing sensitive information and where sensitive data is residing across the enterprise. These analytics may help direct security awareness training and security hardening initiatives, respectively.

9.2.4. Sharing Is Easy

In the same way that using Snowflake as a data platform for security analytics gains from getting data from different sources, in many cases, it's important to share data in a secure way between different teams within and outside of the organization. Using Snowflake, it's easy to share parts of data within the organization (for more information, go to the fine-grained authorization part of Chapter 6, "Authorization: Data Access Control") and outside of your organization (e.g., with reader accounts).

9.3. SnowAlert

Speaking about using Snowflake for security is incomplete without discussing SnowAlert. SnowAlert is an open source security analytics framework that identifies (and alerts on, as the name suggests) security incidents from different data sources and is based on Snowflake. SnowAlert was developed by Snowflake's security team and is continuously updated.

It is based on scheduled queries that are running on log information ingested into Snowflake about system, network, and application events and is quite easy to extend. The application itself runs in a container, and the query results are alerts that are fed into Snowflake tables. These alerts are then standardized to eliminate duplicate entries and suppress repeating alerts, and then notifications are sent to other platforms (such as Jira, Slack, or ServiceNow) so that the right teams can take action based on the alerts.

SnowAlert also lists violations, which are essentially the same as alert information (results of specific queries), but its results require continuous work on risk reduction, rather than "closing an alert." Examples can be found throughout Chapter 7, "Auditing and Monitoring," and include users with lacking authentication strength and other configuration issues. Such data is also written to Snowflake for monitoring by BI tools.

9.3.1. Getting Started

To first get started with SnowAlert, run its docker in installation mode:

```
docker run -it snowsec/snowalert ./install
```

In the first time you run this, as with other docker containers, it will take a while to download the docker, and once it finishes download, you will be asked for

1. Your Snowflake account URL (e.g., acmecandies. snowflakecomputing.com).

2. A username and password for installation (note that you need to use a user with administrative role for SnowAlert installation). Of course, the preferred way is to use SSO, as per Chapter 4, "Authentication: Keeping Strangers Out," of this book.

3. The installation wizard will proceed to create the required database objects, after which it will optionally allow you to create Jira integration and generate an RSA key, for which we recommend to use a randomized key.

4. You will be presented with an environment file command to create. Do so, and run SnowAlert.

9.3.2. Running SnowAlert

Running SnowAlert is done by running the following command:

```
docker run --env-file acmecandies.envs snowsec/snowalert ./run all
```

(replace acmecandies with your account name, it will be displayed at the end of the installation).

You can run this from your laptop or workstation, but you probably want to later on set it to be running from whatever production environment it is that you're using to run containers from. Needless to say, you need to treat the secret key here as every other secret key, as per the key-pair authentication section of Chapter 4, "Authentication: Keeping Strangers Out."

9.3.3. Managing SnowAlert

SnowAlert comes with a web UI to manage its rules and integrations. To run it, run the web UI docker:

```
docker run -it -p 8000:8000 --env-file snowalert-acmecandies.envs
snowsec/snowalert-webui
```

(replace acmecandies with your account name).

You can use `http://localhost:8000` to connect to your SnowAlert web UI server, and from there, you can set up various connectors to security controls (to pull data from), manage the alerts (as well as create new ones), and manage the violations (as well as create new ones).

9.3.4. SnowAlert Data

SnowAlert data is located in your Snowflake account, under the SnowAlert database. You can use SQL queries to query data from it – directly or through a BI or reporting tool. For example, the following query pulls the last ten alerts:

```
SELECT id, alert_time, event_time, title, description
FROM snowalert.data.alerts
ORDER BY alert_time DESC
LIMIT 10;
```

To learn more about SnowAlert, refer to its documentation and github repository.

9.4. Summary

In this chapter, we explored the possibility of using Snowflake for your organization's security analytics. Snowflake has a lot of advantages for doing that, and taking SnowAlert as a platform (from which you can expand) also has its advantages. This was in the introductory chapter, as using or not using Snowflake as a data platform for your security analytics is a lot about what your organization has already invested in, what it uses as a SIEM, what does it use as its main data platform, and more.

Epilogue

Writing a book such as this is challenging. We attempted to strike a balance between not being a book that has a high redundancy with the documentation, a balance between providing "the code you need to solve a problem" and providing the reasoning, a balance between addressing data engineers, security engineers, and other readers. We had a lot of fun writing this book, and we're hoping you had fun reading it and that you found it useful.

Writing a book about a "moving target" such as Snowflake poses another challenge. Since Snowflake didn't decide on a code freeze throughout the writing process, some features were released throughout the writing process, and some were announced but not published yet. We tried to address those, even if the knowledge of such features was obviously limited. This stresses the importance of keeping up to date with any system you're working on. Sometimes a problem you were trying to solve now has a more elegant solution.

By the time you get here, we hope you feel that Snowflake provides a set of great security features and that you're able to move further toward reducing security risks in your Snowflake data cloud. We'd also love to hear feedback from you and how you found the book. We will also continue publishing content around Snowflake security (as we've already done quite extensively before publishing this book).

If you'd like to stay up to date with Snowflake security issues, you're also invited to register with our website `https://snowflake-security.com` to get relevant updates. If you'd like more generic information about DataSecOps, not only around Snowflake, feel free to visit DataSecOps.xyz for information and events around DataSecOps.

© Ben Herzberg, Yoav Cohen 2022
B. Herzberg and Y. Cohen, *Snowflake Security*, https://doi.org/10.1007/978-1-4842-7389-0

Index

© Ben Herzberg, Yoav Cohen 2022
B. Herzberg and Y. Cohen, *Snowflake Security*, https://doi.org/10.1007/978-1-4842-7389-0